Y OWN

OTHER BOOKS AVAILABLE FROM CHILTON

Robbie Fanning, Series Editor

CONTEMPORARY QUILTING SERIES

Appliqué the Ann Boyce Way, by Ann Boyce
Barbara Johannah's Crystal Piecing
Contemporary Quilting Techniques, by Pat Cairns
Fast Patch, by Anita Hallock
Fourteen Easy Baby Quilts, by Margaret Dittman
Machine-Quilted Jackets, Vests, and Coats, by Nancy Moore
Pictorial Quilts, by Carolyn Vosburg Hall
Precision Pieced Quilts Using the Foundation Method, by Jane Hall and Dixie Haywood
Quick-Quilted Home Decor with Your Bernina, by Jackie Dodson
Quick-Quilted Home Decor with Your Sewing Machine, by Jackie Dodson
The Quilter's Guide to Rotary Cutting, by Donna Poster
Quilts by the Slice, by Beckie Olson
Scrap Quilts Using Fast Patch, by Anita Hallock
Speed-Cut Quilts, by Donna Poster
Super Simple Quilts, by Kathleen Eaton
Teach Yourself Machine Piecing and Quilting, by Debra Wagner
Three-Dimensional Appliqué, by Jodie Davis

CRAFT KALEIDOSCOPE SERIES

Creating and Crafting Dolls, by Eloise Piper and Mary Dilligan
Fabric Painting Made Easy, by Nancy Ward
How to Make Cloth Books for Children, by Anne Pellowski
Jane Asher's Costume Book
Quick and Easy Ways with Ribbon, by Ceci Johnson
Learn Bearmaking, by Judi Maddigan
Soft Toys for Babies, by Judi Maddigan
Stamping Made Easy, by Nancy Ward
Too Hot to Handle? Potholders and How to Make Them, by Doris L. Hoover

CREATIVE MACHINE ARTS SERIES

ABCs of Serging, by Tammy Young and Lori Bottom
The Button Lover's Book, by Marilyn Green
Claire Shaeffer's Fabric Sewing Guide
The Complete Book of Machine Embroidery, by Robbie and Tony Fanning
Creative Nurseries Illustrated, by Debra Terry and Juli Plooster
Distinctive Serger Gifts and Crafts, by Naomi Baker and Tammy Young
The Fabric Lover's Scrapbook, by Margaret Dittman
Friendship Quilts by Hand and Machine, by Carolyn Vosburg Hall
Gail Brown's All-New Instant Interiors
Gifts Galore, by Jane Warnick and Jackie Dodson
Hold It! How to Sew Bags, Totes, Duffels, Pouches, and More, by Nancy Restuccia
How to Make Soft Jewelry, by Jackie Dodson
Innovative Serging, by Gail Brown and Tammy Young
Innovative Sewing, by Gail Brown and Tammy Young

The New Creative Serging Illustrated, by Pati Palmer, Gail Brown, and Sue Green
Owner's Guide to Sewing Machines, Sergers, and Knitting Machines, by Gale Grigg Hazen
Petite Pizzazz, by Barb Griffin
Putting on the Glitz, by Sandra L. Hatch and Ann Boyce
Quick Napkin Creations, by Gail Brown
Second Stitches: Recycle as You Sew, by Susan Parker
Serge a Simple Project, by Tammy Young and Naomi Baker
Serged Garments in Minutes, by Tammy Young and Naomi Baker
Sew Any Patch Pocket, by Claire Shaeffer
Sew Any Set-In Pocket, by Claire Shaeffer
Sew Sensational Gifts, by Naomi Baker and Tammy Young
Sew, Serge, Press, by Jan Saunders
Sewing and Collecting Vintage Fashions, by Eileen MacIntosh
Singer Instructions for Art Embroidery and Lace Work
Soft Gardens: Make Flowers with Your Sewing Machine, by Yvonne Perez-Collins
The Stretch & Sew Guide to Sewing Knits, by Ann Person
Twenty Easy Machine-Made Rugs, by Jackie Dodson

KNOW YOUR SEWING MACHINE SERIES, by Jackie Dodson

Know Your Bernina, second edition
Know Your Brother, with Jane Warnick
Know Your Elna, with Carol Ahles
Know Your New Home, with Judi Cull and Vicki Lyn Hastings
Know Your Pfaff, with Audrey Griese
Know Your Sewing Machine
Know Your Singer
Know Your Viking, with Jan Saunders
Know Your White, with Jan Saunders

KNOW YOUR SERGER SERIES, by Tammy Young and Naomi Baker

Know Your baby lock
Know Your Pfaff Hobbylock
Know Your Serger
Know Your White Superlock

STAR WEAR SERIES

Embellishments, by Linda Fry Kenzle
Sweatshirts with Style, by Mary Mulari

TEACH YOURSELF TO SEW BETTER SERIES, by Jan Saunders

A Step-by-Step Guide to Your Bernina
A Step-by-Step Guide to Your New Home
A Step-by-Step Guide to Your Sewing Machine
A Step-by-Step Guide to Your Viking

MAKE IT

YOUR
OWN

Lori Bottom

Ronda Chaney

CHILTON BOOK COMPANY
Radnor, Pennsylvania

Designed by Tracy Baldwin
Cover design by Anthony Jacobson
Cover and interior fashion illustrations by Richard Vyse
Technical illustrations by Laurie Osborne

Manufactured in the United States of America

Library of Congress Cataloging in Publication Data
Bottom, Lori.
    Make it your own / Lori Bottom, Ronda Chaney.
      p.   cm.
    Includes index.
    ISBN 0-8019-8380-0
      1. Dressmaking—Pattern design.   2. Sewing.   I. Chaney, Ronda.
II. Title.
TT520.B68   1994
646.4′072—dc20   94-1491
                                                      CIP

3 4 5 6 7 8 9 0   3 2 1 0 9 8 7 6

Are you interested in a quarterly newsletter about creative uses of the
sewing machine, serger, and knitting machine? Write to The Creative
Machine-s, PO Box 2634, Menlo Park, CA 94026.

CONTENTS

I probably shouldn't admit this, but many of the clothes I make have simple lines and design—something I whip up quickly at the last minute for a trip or event. Seldom do I take the extra time and effort to change the styling or add details to make a garment really unique. But I no longer have an excuse! Here's an easy-to-understand book specifically written to tell someone like me how to fashionably alter or add to patterns to create unique designs with a minimum of time and effort.

Ever since I learned Lori and Ronda were collaborating on *Make It Your Own,* I've been looking forward to reading it and having all of that good information at my fingertips. After having worked with both of them on the *Sewing Update* and *Serger Update* newsletters, I knew this topic was right up their alley. Although they're very busy career women, they have diligently worked on the book over a two-year period and both their creativity and attention to detail certainly shine through.

The excellent first chapter tells how to be your own designer—no matter what your level of experience. Following chapters give simple instructions for interesting collars, necklines, sleeves, overlays, and closures to make your garment one of a kind.

Designers' templates in the book's appendix are a big help for sketching new styles. You can keep the proportions accurate and get a good idea of how a design detail will look before cutting out your garment.

With this book, I'm sure I'll sew more creatively. However, I now have a new problem—deciding which of all these terrific design details to add to my next projects!

Tammy Young

ACKNOWLEDGMENTS

We would like to extend a very special thank you to our artists, Richard Vyse and Laurie Osborne. Richard created all the fashion art throughout the book, including the line drawings, cover illustrations, and inside color pages. His sense of design and fashion and his attention to detail amazed us time and time again as each new chapter was completed. Laurie created all the technical line drawings throughout the book. As an avid sewer, Laurie's knowledge of garment construction was a definite asset to creating clarity throughout the illustrations. Both Richard and Laurie went far beyond our expectations and their contribution was invaluable.

The following are registered trademark names used in this book: *Fasturn*, *Loop Turner*, *Scotch Magic*, *Ultraleather*, and *Ultrasuede*.

A student once told Ronda, "Thanks for giving me the courage and guidance to escape from the limited styling of commercial patterns to create my own designs." We wrote *Make It Your Own* because we, too, have a passion for sewing one-of-a-kind garments. In this book, we'd like to show you how you can take a basic pattern and easily turn it into hundreds of original designs with just a few simple pattern adjustments. You'll be amazed at the freedom this allows for endless creative options, while at the same time it's easier and faster than drafting a pattern from the start, and much more fun than following the exact guidelines of a pattern.

Because we both have families and full-time jobs, as well as our writing on the side, sewing time is at a premium. As much as we may enjoy drafting patterns from scratch, we do not always have the time. Not willing to compromise on style and wanting to use the best design opportunities to create our own garments, we like to concentrate on making simple modifications to existing patterns.

Changing a collar or the front of a jacket, reshaping a neckline, securing tabs or ties across the back of a full coat, or inserting lace down the center of a sleeve are just a few easy adjustments that can transform an ordinary pattern into a unique and custom design. When designing with details, even a beginning sewer can be her own designer.

Although we had a wonderful time playing with fabric to come up with the details and design options throughout this book, we hope that these will only be a springboard for your own creative process. Planning the garment and the creative process can be as much fun as wearing the garment.

Here are suggestions on how to make the most of *Make It Your Own:*

■ *Read the first chapter,* our favorite, because it's all about the creative process. Reread it any time you feel discouraged, need some creative inspiration, or lack incentive for those stale sewing projects. Make time for the creativity exercises—just reading them is not enough; you must experience them to realize their true value. You'll love the refreshing release they provide to a busy, frantic schedule.

■ *Flip through the remaining chapters,* looking at the fashion illustrations for favorite options. The chapters are organized by garment areas, such as collars, necklines, sleeves, fabric overlays, or closures. Each chapter includes step-by-step instructions for several design details. Because each detail is independent from the others, you may read about them in any order (page numbers are indicated for any cross references).

■ *Choose a detail that catches your eye.* Each detail includes: "Pattern and Design Considerations," which give fabric and pattern tips as well as instructions for any pattern adjustments needed; "Construction Steps," which give step-by-step instructions to execute the detail; and for some details, we've included "Endless Options," which give ideas for unique variations.

■ *Notice the "Design & Sew Tips."* They explain special techniques that may be valuable in creating the most satisfactory touches to the design detail.

■ *Refer to a general sewing reference book.* We recommend that you keep a good all-around basic sewing manual in your sewing library. If there are construction terms in this book that you are not familiar with, please read about them in your basic sewing guide. We have concentrated on how to customize patterns for creative design and, therefore, were not able to define more fundamental construction techniques such as grading or understitching. Whether you are a beginning sewer or have many years of experience

working with fashion, fabric, and patterns, we are confident you will find our design ideas and construction techniques easy to follow.

■ *Use the "Designers' Templates" in the Appendix.* These blank figure drawings allow you to practice sketching garment designs while keeping proportions accurate. Designing with a pencil before carrying it to fabric is invaluable. Create as daring or outrageous designs as you like without taking the risk or incurring the costs of making a design you don't like. Photocopy the templates, leaving the book unmarked so you'll always have a fresh template to copy from.

■ *Have fun being your own designer!* We're confident that you'll come up with additional creative ideas of your own. These may be variations of the details in this book or completely new options. Remember to go back to chapter 1 for a creative refresher.

In the process of writing this book, we experienced the enjoyment and productivity of designing with each other. Yes, we had a fantastic experience working together, and at the same time, we felt as though that fellowship contributed to the creative process. Although we won't meet all of you in person, we hope reading this book will help provide that same productivity of sewing with a friend.

Your Sewing Friends,

Lori and *Ronda*

CHAPTER 1

YOU, THE DESIGNER

How do you respond when someone tells you how creative you are? Some may say "Me? You must have the wrong person" or "Not me, I just follow the pattern guidesheet." Although you may not agree at first, we believe you are creative and we'd like to show you. With a little guidance and the willingness to try, you're on your way to *Make It Your Own*.

Be sure to do the creativity exercises (described throughout this chapter). Although some of them may seem unusual, we challenge you to relax and have fun with them. Only after you practice the exercises will you understand how they add confidence to the creative process and develop a new level of awareness, a creative release that we, as well as many others, have experienced.

■ THE FABRIC OF CREATIVITY

Did you know that the inspiration for Velcro® was the small prickly thistle balls produced as seedpods on cocklebur bushes? A Swiss mountaineer became frustrated by the burs that clung annoyingly to his pants and socks. While picking them off, he realized that it might be possible to produce a fastener based on the burs to compete with the zipper. The success of his "locking tape" is well known today. Observing the world with fresh eyes allows you to give novel meaning to something seemingly ordinary. This means letting go of judgments or preconceived ideas so you can visualize a unique application or an unusual resolution.

Creativity is a new way of looking at the world. It's a skill anyone can learn and practice. The lockstitch sewing machine was invented by Elias Howe. He had worked on the machine intensely for many years and was not successful until a dream presented him with the idea for the machine needle to have the open eye near the point. In his early attempts, he had placed the hole in the middle of the needle shank. The successful answer came as he slept.

For now, consider the creative process just for the sake of being creative. Forget about fabric, construction details, patterns, or end results. To prepare yourself, consider these exercises to get you started thinking creatively.

✎ *Through the Eyes of a Child*—Seeing like a child can be a freeing and motivating experience. Inhibitions are removed and, for the first time in a long while, we may be able to see things with a fresh new perspective. Go to a neighborhood pool or playground and watch the children play; watch them experiment; notice their fearlessness, their trust, and their honesty. There is a little child in everyone. Think back to the child in yourself; remember how easy it was to plunge in and make clothes for your dolls or how much fun it was just to play with buttons and make outlines of shapes? Encourage the child in yourself and, in turn, nurture your own creativity.

✎ *Habits, Diminishing or Productive*—Shopping lists, organized file drawers, and lunch at noon are all important habits that help us get through the day. Sometimes, however, those seemingly irrelevant habits can block creativity. They act as a blindfold that keeps us from seeking out simple, but significant, alternatives. Perhaps that's why our most creative friends may seem a bit eccentric or unrealistic.

Make a list of all the familiar things you do out of habit. Carry the list around with you throughout the day and add to it as you think of additional routines. When your list is fairly complete, go through each habit one-by-one and try the task a new way. Take your time working through the list; perhaps revise one task a week. Have fun with this, even if it may be impractical. You'll become more aware of your habits, perhaps think of more effective and efficient routines, and enhance your creativity all at the time same time.

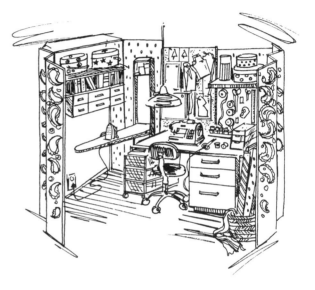

■ Looking for Inspiration?

Inspiration is in every direction. With no limits to creativity, let the shapes, colors, and textures around you contribute to the designs in your mind. Fashion need not be inspired only by fashion. Fashion designers often get their ideas from events, movies, art, the environment, or politics. Kaffe Fasset, world famous for his knitting and needlepoint designs, transfers shapes and colors from sources such as bird eggs or a pottery vase to his wonderful textile designs.

✎ *Imagery*—As you look at nature, fabric, food, or whatever inspires you to be creative, hold the images of the items in your mind. (You may also remember images from dreams.) Choose one or more items that you think are particularly beautiful in their own way; they don't have to, and probably won't, relate to fashion. Keep the item(s) in your mind as you go about your daily tasks. Eventually some of the images will appear to you as design possibilities. Imagery can be very powerful in any of your artistic endeavors.

✎ *Increased Awareness*—Pick an object, any object, and observe it for a set period of time. Ten minutes may be enough, or if you can concentrate longer, set a longer time span. As you look at the object, think about how some part of it could be incorporated into clothing. Perhaps the color, shape, texture, or lines will contribute to your clothing image.

A student reply to this awareness exercise: *I focused on the clouds in the evening sky as I took my daily walk. Shapes and colors came and went as the clouds moved. The shapes were often asymmetrical to match my personality and my design preferences. Nature's colors are always perfect and harmonize so beautifully together. When I thought I had seen all the colors, I took off my sunglasses and the colors changed again. I had new ideas for putting fabric colors together.*

✎ *Observation*—Take a measuring tape, pad of paper, and pencil or pen and go outside. Lay the tape down, forming a circle over any surface (Fig. 1-1). Stay completely quiet and observe everything in the circle for 20 minutes. After the time is up, write down everything you saw or felt. Surprisingly, 20 minutes may not be enough time. The more you look, the more you'll see. Repeat this exercise regularly. This way of seeing is ideal for enhancing your creativity.

One student had the following response to the observation exercise: *I went into the back-yard and stared at a gravel area near a wooden ramp. After sitting for a while, I saw that each piece of granite gravel had a pattern that could*

FIG. 1-1. Form a circle with your measuring tape over any surface, then quietly observe everything within it. Draw or write down what you saw and felt.

be used as a fabric print or textile surface. All the gravel pieces together also made a unique pattern. The way the waterproofing rubbed off the ramp made a design. The way the paint chipped off in strips on the board made a pattern. Even the spider webs clinging onto the ramp could be used to make a beautiful print. What a discovery to know I have such inspiration in just a small part of my backyard!

■ Capturing Creativity

By now, you've probably discovered many sources of inspiration. Here are some tips and activities to help you turn that inspiration into creativity:

■ *Be Disciplined*—Creativity can be hard work and takes concentration. A preplanned time frame is often helpful. Many artists or designers set aside the same time every day to create. They stick to that time even if it proves unproductive. Seemingly unproductive periods can actually be very constructive. You may not be able to plan creative time every day, but perhaps once a week is more fitting to your lifestyle.

Planning a time-frame will help slow down your ideas so you can actually be productive with them. If you're in a hurry or if the ideas come too fast, it's difficult to convert them into a design.

✎ *Scheduled Creativity*—Set aside some creative time once a week. Write it on your calendar and stick to it.

■ *Set Goals*—Channel your creativity by setting goals. Let your goals grow as you grow. To begin with, your goals may be to practice the exercises in this book. Then you may want to convert those images to fashion. (We'll learn more about converting images to fashion later in this chapter.) Perhaps your goals will be to design a fashion detail and make a test sample or integrate it into a garment, or perhaps there's a particular design challenge that you want to resolve.

✎ *Creative Goal Setting*—Set a personal goal that's right for you. Be sure to write it down. Write specifically what it is you want to accomplish and by what date you want to accomplish it. Put it where you'll see it often, perhaps on your calendar or even on your bathroom mirror.

■ *Value Mistakes*—Believe it or not, mistakes or roadblocks can be very beneficial. They cause us to search for a different, and often better, way. They facilitate experimentation with new materials, techniques, or styles. Mistakes or challenges are an important part

of the process because they provide unique opportunities for creativity.

California designer John Marshall made the mistake of creating a design where bias-grain fabric was stitched to straight-grain fabric, causing a puckered seam. To "correct" the mistake, he made an all-over puckering design.

■ *Temporarily Let Go*—When you have a creative block or can't find a resolution to a problem, there comes a time when it may be more productive to stop working on that project. After struggling with an idea without making progress, let go of it and do something else. Go for a walk, go out with friends, paint your nails, or take a bath. While you have consciously stopped thinking about the problem, your mind is still working on it. Sometimes we get too close to a situation and can't see the resolution; however, when we step back, there is room for clarity.

■ *Enjoy the Process*—Don't forget the reason why you're doing this. Is this your hobby, your career, your creative release, your personal time for indulgence? Even if your concentration is on the end product (perhaps a beautiful dress), don't forget to have fun with the process. Edith Head once said, "If everyone was born with the ability to sew, no one would need a therapist."

■ FROM CREATIVITY TO FASHION

Fabrics, trims, buttons, and embellishments are among our favorite mediums for expressing creativity. There's something particularly special and rewarding about designing and wearing your own creations. Garments speak a language; they are an extension of yourself, expressing personality, aspirations, moods, and talent. When you know you look great, it's only natural to feel positive about yourself.

The previous creativity exercises are fun and

productive in their own way, and you'll want to go back and repeat them on a regular basis. However, from a practical perspective, you may be asking yourself how to convert those creative ideas to actual garment designs. We've put together some ideas and exercises to get you started.

■ Practical Considerations

One of our goals in writing this book is to show that you don't have to be an expert sewer to be your own designer. With simple pattern modifications, you can create your own details. When combined with the ideal fabric and pattern selections, you can have a garment personalized to your own creative visions.

We've included step-by-step instructions for implementing the details throughout this book; so if you're a little shaky about straying from the pattern guidesheet, follow the design ideas exactly as we have described them here. When you get more confident, consider varying the details with ideas from the "Endless Options" sections or come up with your own variations.

■ ROOM FOR NEW IDEAS

Here's a good way to stop feeling guilty about those half completed projects or ready-made clothes that you purchased and never wore.

✎ *No More Spider Webs*—Clean out your closet. Set aside a few hours and take everything out of your closet. Put back only those garments that are wonderful, look great on, fit perfectly, are well-made, or whatever other qualities make them stand out for you.

Stand back and take a good look at what's in your closet. Don't be discouraged if there are only a few garments in there. "Less is more" is a statement we think applies appropriately to a fashion wardrobe. Make a list of what you have and what qualities you like most about

each garment. Then make a list of wardrobe "holes," the additions you need to make your wardrobe complete. The list of holes is a good place to begin when thinking about practical applications for your creative ideas. The list of desirable qualities is also helpful in choosing favorable fabrics, colors, and styles.

Now, evaluate those garments you took out of the closet. Give away those garments you haven't worn for over a year. Survey each garment that you have left. What are the redeeming qualities and what are the negative qualities? Can you change a hemline, vary the buttons, or do some mending to improve the garment's appeal? Some of the projects in this book can be done to ready-made garments; perhaps adding a detail or varying a sleeve will give the garment the attention it needs. Consider giving away those garments that just don't look good on you; they may work wonders for someone else. Put back those garments that you need but can't yet replace.

■ HELPFUL TOOLS

Listed below are some of the tools that will help make some of the techniques described throughout this book easier to perform.

PATTERNMAKING TOOLS
Pencils and erasers for pattern drawing and sketching.
Rulers (straight and curved) for drawing accurate and pleasantly shaped lines.
French curve for drawing a variety of curves.
Yardstick (metal or wood) for drawing and measuring extended lines.
T-square and L-square for accurate corners or perpendicular lines.
Pattern paper or wrapping tissue for making patterns.
Measuring tape for pattern work and construction.
Transparent tape for slash and spread pattern adjustments.

Tag board (manila folders) for making templates or for repeating a shape on an edge (such as a scalloped edge).

Compass for drawing circles or curves.

Scissors for cutting paper (paper will dull fabric shears).

CONSTRUCTION TOOLS

Tracing wheel and carbon, chalk, and disappearing marking pens for marking.

Plastic or bamboo point turner for turning perfect corners.

Bent-handle dressmaker's shears for cutting fabric.

Six-inch sewing gauge for easy measuring of small areas.

Long straight pins with large heads for pinning all fabric types.

Hand sewing needles and machine needles in a variety of sizes for sewing all fabric types.

Loop Turner or Fasturn for turning fabric tubes right side out.

PRESSING TOOLS

Steam iron for pressing and shaping fabric and setting stitches at all stages of construction.

Tailor's ham for pressing shaped areas and curved seams.

Seam roll for pressing seam allowances open and pressing seams in narrow areas.

Clapper for pressing sharp creases without an over-pressed look.

Wooden point press for pressing corners and points, and pressing straight seams open.

Tailor's board with a variety of shaped edges for pressing curved seams.

Press cloths for protecting the right side of the fabric during pressing.

■ RESOURCES

Following are a few mail-order resources that carry a number of the tools listed above.

Clotilde, Inc., 1909 SW First Ave., Ft. Lauderdale, FL 33315, 305-761-8655.

Nancy's Notions, Ltd., 333 Beichl Ave., P.O. Box 683, Beaver Dam, WI 53916-0683, 1-800-833-0690.

Sew/Fit Co., 5768 W. 77th, Burbank, IL 60459, 708-458-5600.

The Fabric Carr, P.O. Box 32120, San Jose, CA, 95152, 408-929-1651.

■ Immerse Yourself

In a previous section, we concentrated on creative inspiration from non-fashion sources. Here we encourage you to immerse yourself in fashion (Fig. 1-2). The best way to develop an eye for fashion is to become intimately familiar with what's available. Allow yourself plenty of time for this and be consistent about exposing yourself to fashion on a regular basis. This is an important and ongoing step in the creative process. Here are some of our ideas for fashion

FIG. 1-2. For creative inspiration, immerse yourself in fashion.

inspiration, but we're sure you'll have your personal favorites too.

High-priced boutiques and department stores

Out-of-the-way, funky boutiques—You'd be amazed at the wealth of ideas in these shops

Ethnic shops, such as Chinatown stores or Indian sari shops

Second-hand stores

Fashion magazines, such as *Women's Wear Daily, Vogue, or* catalog shopping

Sewing publications, such as *Sew News, Threads, Sewing Update,* and *Serger Update*

Historic costume books—Often available at your local library or a college bookstore (with a fashion department)

Old-fashioned magazines—One of our favorite inspirations, look for these at garage sales and flea markets

Newspapers—Politics have a prominent influence on fashion trends

✎ *Fashion Story Board*—Make a large bulletin board in your sewing room or office and tack to it anything that inspires you (Fig. 1-3). It could be a collage of clippings from magazines and catalogs; a sketch of a favorite garment; fabric swatches, trims, or buttons that coordinate perfectly; or a pattern envelope with unique styling. Add to and change the board regularly. Match fabrics to a garment sketch or catalog clipping, or create a particular mood with a collection of garment ideas combined with just the right fabric swatches.

✎ *Fashion Idea Notebook*—Gather a collection of clippings, sketches, photos, or photocopies of favorite garments. Use a binder, file box, photo album, or notebook, whatever is most inspiring for you (Fig. 1-4). Organize the notebook by types of garments or details, such as separate sections for collars, sleeves, pockets, and hems. Your notebook will be constantly evolving just as fashion does. Update it often, removing those ideas that aren't as inspiring and adding new outrageous styles.

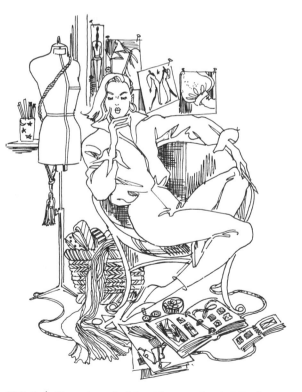

FIG. 1-3. Tack fashion clippings or drawings, fabric swatches, trims, and buttons to a bulletin board to create your own fashion story board.

FIG. 1-4. Organize a fashion idea notebook full of your favorite sketches, photos, clippings, and fabric swatches.

■ Moving Forward

Now that you've cleaned out your closet, gathered a collection of helpful tools, and filled your mind with creative inspiration, it's time to begin designing and constructing garments that suit your own style. We recommend that you begin designing with a pencil and paper.

✎ *Sketch, Sketch, Sketch*—There's no risk involved in a sketch. If it doesn't look good, just turn the page and start again. Drawing a sketch is the best way to find out if a particular neckline shape goes with a unique style sleeve, or if a dress would be more proportionately balanced short or long.

   If you're not much of an artist when it comes to drawing figures, photocopy the Designers' Templates in the Appendix of this book. The Designers' Templates are outline sketches of a figure, including both a front and back view template. Use them to sketch your garment while maintaining accurate figure proportions. Leave the templates in the book unmarked so you'll always have a fresh template to copy. Copy them as many times as you like.

✎ *Adapting Ready-to-Wear Ideas*—While you're shopping the stores and catalogs, make a note of any details or design ideas you might consider duplicating. Look closely at the construction, shapes and curves, and proportion of the detail. Draw a sketch of the detail and write down as many notes as you can remember. (We recommend you do your sketching after you leave the shop; it's a bit more courteous.) Sketch the detail over and over again, varying the shape and design of the garment, as well as the positioning and shape of the detail.

When you've sketched the garment design you want, the next step is to shop the pattern catalogs. Look for the pattern that is the closest to the garment style in your sketch. While paging through the catalogs, you may want to update your sketch with a new styling that you prefer, or perhaps you'll find one pattern with a sleeve you want and another pattern with the right bodice styling.

Carefully study the pattern(s) and their directions; make a construction game plan for any modifications you want to make to the pattern. Follow the guidelines throughout the rest of this book to modify particular details such as the neckline shape, the closure, or the collar detail. When planning your design, consider the type of care that will be needed for the fabric as well as any details to be incorporated into the garment. Inner construction such as shoulder pads, interfacing, lining, or underlining, as well as outer details such as topstitching thread, trims, buttons, and closures will affect the finished garment care methods. As you modify patterns to create your own designs, be sure to allow for any additional yardage requirements from those indicated on the pattern envelope. For example, if fullness and flare are added to a garment design, you will need to recalculate the yardage specifications. If using expensive fabric, you may want to make pattern adjustments first, then lay out your pattern and calculate yardage requirements before purchasing your fabric.

CHAPTER 2

COLLAR COLLECTIONS

Changing or adding a collar is an easy way to vary the entire look of a garment. You can start with a basic pattern and make a striking garment by adding a dramatic collar. This chapter gives ideas for reshaping collars or creating your own unique collar pattern. For added variety, you can always reshape the neckline before creating the collar pattern. If you're unsure of the finished look or want to practice a new construction method, we recommend you make a sample out of muslin before cutting into the fashion fabric.

■ CUSTOMIZED COLLAR SHAPES

FIG. 2-1. Customized collar shapes.

Design your own novelty collar by reshaping the outside collar edge (Fig. 2-1). Modify an existing flat-collar pattern, or create one from scratch. The inside seamline of a flat collar has the same shape as the garment neckline. As a result, the collar does not roll. This makes creating a collar pattern easy, and allows for endless collar shapes and sizes.

■ PATTERN AND DESIGN CONSIDERATIONS

1. Use the Designers' Templates in the Appendix to experiment with various collar shapes. Draw the neckline shape first, then sketch the collar shape. Be sure the front and back collars are the same width at the shoulders. Allow for a garment closure by positioning the collar opening at the closure.

2. Creating a collar pattern: (If you are modifying an existing flat collar, skip this step and go directly to Step 3.) To create the collar pattern, overlap the front and back bodice patterns at the shoulder seamline. Position the patterns so the shoulder seamlines overlap ½″ at the armscye and line up at the neckline (Fig. 2-2). This will remove extra

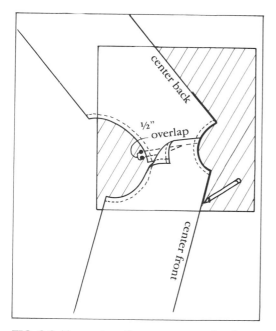

FIG. 2-2. To create collar pattern, overlap front and back patterns at shoulder seams. Match seams at neckline and overlap ½″ at armscye. Trace center front, center back, and neckline.

fullness from the outside collar edge for a better fitting collar. Trace the neckline (seamline and cutting line). Unless making an asymmetrical design, you only need to draft half the collar; it will then be cut on the fold or in two pieces so the right and left sides are identical.

>⸰ N O T E : If desired, you may adjust the neckline shape before drafting the collar. (See "Reshaping the Neckline," page 37.)

3. Drafting a facing pattern: If your pattern doesn't already have a facing piece of if you have changed the shape of the neckline, you need to draw a new facing pattern using the bodice pattern as a guide. See the Design and Sew Tip for *Drafting a Facing Pattern* on page 39.

4. Shaping the collar pattern (Fig. 2-3): Using your template sketch as a guide, draw the outside edge of the collar, creating the desired collar width and shape. If making repetitive shapes (such as for a scalloped edge), fold the pattern accordion style or use a cardboard template so the shape is duplicated exactly. Be sure to draft both the front and back sides, and allow for the garment closure (if there is one) by positioning the collar opening at the closure as shown in Figure 2-3.

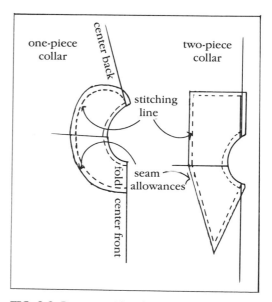

FIG. 2-3. Draw outside edge of collar pattern with desired collar width and shape.

5. Add seam allowances to the outside edge(s). If the collar will be one piece, mark the foldline at the center front or center back.

■ **CONSTRUCTION STEPS**

1. Cut the upper and under collars from fashion fabric, and one from interfacing. Attach the interfacing to the upper collar.
2. Stitch the upper and under collars right sides together along the outside edge(s). Trim and clip the seam allowances as needed, then turn the collar right side out. Press the collar flat, rolling the seamline toward the under collar.
3. Cut the facing from fashion fabric. Stitch the facing shoulder seams, then finish the outside edge.
4. Construct the garment following the pattern guidesheet, leaving the neckline unfinished. Baste the collar to the neckline with the under collar toward the right side of the garment.
5. Pin the facing to the neckline, with the right side of the facing toward the upper collar. Turn the facing edges to the wrong side at the closure (Fig. 2-4). Stitch the neckline through all layers.
6. Trim and clip the seam allowances, press the facing to the inside of the garment, and understitch the facing to the seam allowances. Hand tack the facing at the shoulder seams and closure (if there is one).

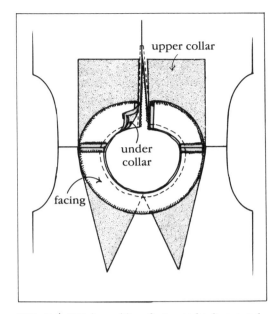

FIG. 2-4. Stitch neckline facing to bodice, sandwiching collar. Turn facing edges to wrong side at closure.

■ SHOULDER-SEAM COLLAR

FIG. 2-5. Shoulder-seam collar.

This collar is applied to the front of the garment, then stitched into the shoulder seam (or yoke seam). Reshape the outside edge of the collar for a custom look (Fig. 2-5).

■ PATTERN AND DESIGN CONSIDERATIONS

Begin with a blouse or dress pattern and, if desired, adjust the shape of the neckline (see "Reshaping the Neckline," beginning on page 37). Use the bodice front pattern to create a flat collar pattern for the front portion of the garment (Fig. 2-6). Trace the neckline and shoulder seam, then draw the outside edge of the collar. If the pattern doesn't have a facing or if you've changed the neckline shape, use the Design and Sew Tip on page 39, *Drafting a Facing Pattern*.

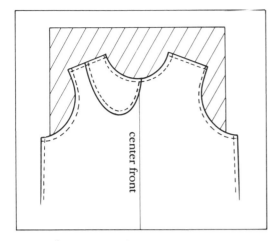

FIG. 2-6. Use bodice-front pattern to create a flat collar pattern for front of garment.

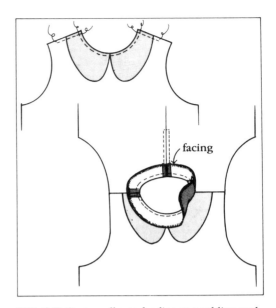

FIG. 2-7. Baste collar to bodice at neckline and shoulders. Join front and back at shoulders, and stitch facing to neckline.

■ CONSTRUCTION STEPS

1. Cut the upper and under collars from fashion fabric and cut one from interfacing. Attach the interfacing to the upper collar and stitch the upper and under collars right sides together along the outside edges.

✂ N O T E : So that the seamline will roll to the underside, decrease the outside edge of the under collar by ⅛″.

2. Trim and clip the seam allowances, turn the collar right side out, and press.

3. Baste the raw edges of the collar to the bodice front at the neckline and shoulder seamlines. Join the front and back at the shoulders (Fig. 2-7).

4. Cut the facing from fashion fabric. Stitch the facing at the shoulder seams and finish the outside edge.

5. Position the facing to the garment at the neckline with right sides together, turning the facing ends to the wrong side at the closure (if there is one). Stitch the neckline edges through all layers as shown in Figure 2-7.

6. Trim and clip the allowances, press the facing to the wrong side, and understitch the facing to the seam allowances. Tack the facing at the shoulder seams and closure (if there is one). Complete the garment following the pattern guidesheet.

REVERSE-FACING COLLAR

FIG. 2-8. Reverse-facing collar.

This collar is not actually a collar in the traditional sense; it's simply a reversed facing that is shaped to look like a collar. It's a cinch to make and a few variations will provide countless creative options (Fig. 2-8).

■ PATTERN AND DESIGN CONSIDERATIONS

1. Begin with a blouse or dress pattern. Eliminate the collar and neckline facing pieces if there are any.
2. To make the front collar pattern, trace the neckline, shoulder, and center-front lines of the bodice-front pattern (Fig. 2-9). If creating

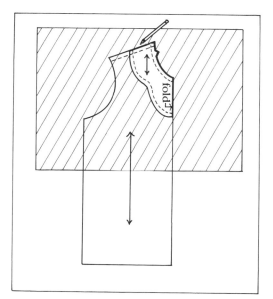

FIG. 2-9. To make collar pattern, trace bodice at neckline, shoulder, and center front. Draw outside collar edge creating desired shape.

an asymmetrical collar or if the garment has an asymmetrical neckline, be sure to trace both the right and left sides of the bodice.

3. Draw the outside line of the collar, creating the desired shape. Experiment by varying the

collar shape, or create more than one collar piece and partially overlap them (Fig. 2-10). Use the Designers' Templates in the Appendix to experiment with various collar shapes.

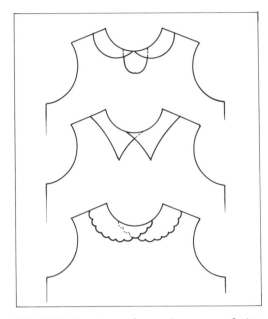

FIG. 2-10. Experiment by varying reverse-facing collar shapes and overlapping collar pieces.

4. Add seam allowances to the outside edges and transfer the grainline, notches, or other markings. If you're going to bind the outside edge, there's no need to add seam allowances.

5. Repeat Steps 2 through 4 to create the back collar pattern. Be sure the front and back are the same width at the shoulder seam.

■ **CONSTRUCTION STEPS**

1. Cut the collar from complementary fabric. You may cut the collar on the straight or bias grainline.

2. Stitch the shoulder seams of the collar, then stitch the shoulder seams of the garment.

Complete the garment closure, following the pattern guidesheet.

✂ N O T E : For button closures, sew the buttonholes and attach the buttons after attaching the collar.

3. Hem or bind the outside edge of the collar (Fig. 2-11).

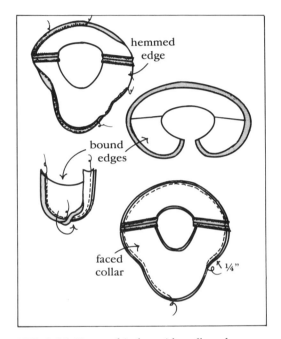

FIG. 2-11. Hem or bind outside collar edge, or face with a second collar piece.

▷ O P T I O N A L : Another option is to face the collar. Cut two of each collar piece and seam the outside edges right sides together. Trim the seam to ¼″ and clip the allowances if needed. Turn the collar right side out and press. Continue the procedure, treating the two layers as one.

4. Stitch the right side of the collar to the wrong side of the garment at the neckline (Fig. 2-12). Grade and clip the seam allowances. Then turn the collar to the right side of the garment and press.

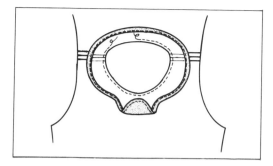

FIG. 2-12. Stitch right side of collar to wrong side of neckline.

▷ OPTIONAL: Instead of stitching the collar to the neckline as above, trim off the neckline seam allowances. Then place the wrong side of the collar to the right side of the garment neckline. Baste them together at the neckline and bind the neckline edge, as for the collar shown in Figure 2-13.

5. Pin the collar in place along the outside edge. Edgestitch or hand blindstitch the outside edge of the collar to the garment.

FIG. 2-13. Reverse-facing collar with neckline and collar edges bound.

■ YOKE COLLAR

FIG. 2-14. Yoke collar.

This technique is actually a yoke that is made to imitate a collar. Shape the yoke as desired for an ideal collar line. Use contrasting fabrics for the best effect. Give added detail by adding trim, piping, or topstitching to the yoke seam (Fig. 2-14).

■ PATTERN AND DESIGN
CONSIDERATIONS

1. Start with any dress or blouse pattern that has a faced neckline. If desired, adjust the neckline shape before making yoke modifications (see Reshaping the Neckline, page 37).

2. Use the Designers' Templates in the Appendix to experiment with different yoke lines. Draw the desired yoke-collar line onto the bodice front and back patterns (Fig. 2-15). Be sure the front and back yoke lines meet at the shoulder seam. If desired, you can make a yoke collar on just the front bodice with no changes to the back of the garment.

3. Mark the grainline on the yoke and draw notches for accurate matching. Cut the bodice pattern apart along the yoke-collar line. Add ¼″ seam allowances to both edges as shown in Figure 2-15.

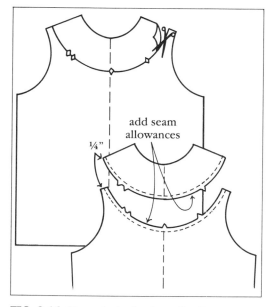

FIG. 2-15. Draw desired yoke-collar line onto front and back bodice patterns. Mark grainline and notches. Cut pattern apart and add seam allowances.

■ CONSTRUCTION STEPS

1. Cut the yoke and bodice from contrasting fabric. Staystitch the bodice along the curved seamline, then clip the curve to the stitching (Fig. 2-16).

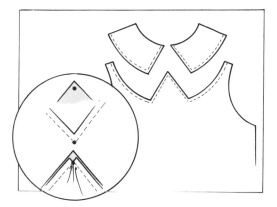

FIG. 2-16. Stitch yoke to bodice, pulling inside bodice curve to fit outside yoke curve.

2. Stitch the yoke to the bodice, pulling the inside curve of the bodice to fit the outside curve of the yoke. Press the allowances toward the yoke collar.

3. Construct the garment following the pattern guidesheet, using the bodice front and back with the newly added yoke.

ENDLESS OPTIONS
For a slightly different look, leave the bodice pattern intact instead of making a separate yoke piece. Then topstitch the wrong side of the collar piece to the right side of the bodice. Construct the garment, treating the collar and bodice pieces as one. Use facing or binding to finish the neckline edge.

◼ DRAPED-PLEAT COLLAR

FIG. 2-17. Draped-pleat collar.

Here's an example of a collar you can create by
adding a pleat and varying the outside edge.
We saw similar collar styling on a very expensive ready-to-wear blouse (Fig. 2-17). Use a
light- to medium-weight supple fabric that
drapes well.

■ PATTERN AND DESIGN CONSIDERATIONS

1. Use a blouse or dress pattern with a pointed collar; wider collars add a more dramatic effect. We used a flat collar, but a collar with a slight roll will also work. Extend the center front of the collar pattern by taping an 8″ square of pattern paper to the front edge.
2. Fold the pattern back along the front seamline. Draw the collar extension using the measurements shown (Fig. 2-18). To draw the extension measure 3″ along the neck seamline beginning at the center front. From this point, draw a line perpendicular to the neck seamline; the length of this line is equal to the collar's center front (A) plus 2″. Unfold the extension and add seam allowances.

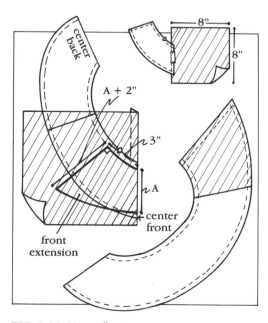

FIG. 2-18. Tape 8″ square of pattern paper to front edge of collar. Fold pattern back at front seamline and draw extension. Unfold extension and add seam allowances.

■ CONSTRUCTION STEPS

1. Cut two collars of fabric and one of interfacing. Use a soft, stitchable interfacing such as silk organza or cotton batiste.
2. Interface the upper collar. Then stitch the upper and under collars right sides together along the outside and front edges. Trim the seam allowances and turn the collar right side out. Edge-stitch if desired.
3. Pin a 1½″ pleat in each front edge, folding the fabric toward the under collar (Fig. 2-19). Baste the pleats at the neckline edge.

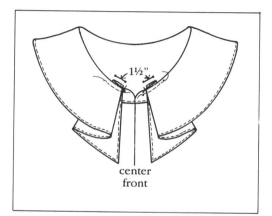

FIG. 2-19. Fold pleats toward under collar and baste.

4. Construct the blouse, following the pattern guidesheet. Before attaching the collar, pin it to the garment and try on the blouse to see if the pleats hang correctly. Remove the basting and readjust the pleats if needed.

ENDLESS OPTIONS

Consider eliminating the interfacing for added drape, or make the collar single layer and serge-finish or satin-zigzag the outside edge.

■ BOW COLLAR

FIG. 2-20. Bow collar.

Make a simple fashion statement with this cre-ative-collar addition (Fig. 2-20). Use lightweight contrast fabric for the bow. Crisp fabric, such as organdy, holds sharp pleats at the bow center, whereas supple fabrics create a graceful drape with soft gathers at the center.

■ PATTERN AND DESIGN CONSIDERATIONS

Choose a blouse or dress pattern with a back closure and a simple rounded neckline. Trace the neckline and shoulder edges. Draw the out-side edge of the collar, beginning at the shoul-der 3″ from the neckline (Fig. 2-21). Draw the sides of the collar straight down parallel to the grainline for 10″. Adjust the size of the collar if desired, then add seam allowances to the out-side edges.

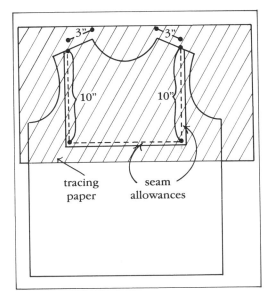

FIG. 2-21. Make collar pattern by tracing bodice neckline and shoulder edges, then draw outside collar edge.

■ CONSTRUCTION STEPS

1. You can make the collar double layer with an upper and under collar or single layer with hemmed or bound edges. Cut one or two collars depending on the finish you're using.

> ✂ N O T E : So that the seamline will roll to the underside of a double-layer collar, decrease the outside edge of the undercollar by ⅛″.

2. Cut a 5″ by 3″ rectangle from matching or contrasting fabric for a loop to hold the center of the bow. Fold the strip in half lengthwise right sides together and stitch a ¼″ seam. Turn the loop right side out and press.

3. For a double-layer collar, stitch the upper and under collars right sides together at the outside edges. Grade the seam allowances and clip the corners. Turn the collar rightside out and press. For a single-layer collar, hem or bind the outside edges as desired and press.

4. Position one end of the loop to the center front of the garment at the neckline edge, right sides together. Position the wrong side of the collar to the right side of the garment with the loop sandwiched between (Fig. 2-22). Baste the layers together at the shoulder and neckline edges.

5. Pull the loose end of the loop around the outside edge of the collar, causing the collar to gather or pleat at the center. Pin or baste the remaining end of the loop in place.

6. Sew the front and back bodice right sides together at the shoulder seams, catching the bow collar in the stitching.

7. Seam the front and back facings at the shoulders. Position the facing to the neckline edge of the garment right sides together. Turn the facing ends to the wrong side at the back closure. Stitch the neckline edges through all layers.

8. Trim and clip the allowances, press the facing to the wrong side, and understitch the facing to the allowances. Complete the garment following the pattern guidesheet.

ENDLESS OPTIONS

For variation, extend the collar pattern to the armscye and make the outside collar edge round instead of square (Fig. 2-23).

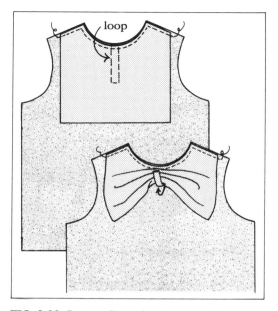

FIG. 2-22. Baste collar to bodice at neckline and shoulder edges with loop sandwiched between. Pull loose end of loop around collar and baste at neckline.

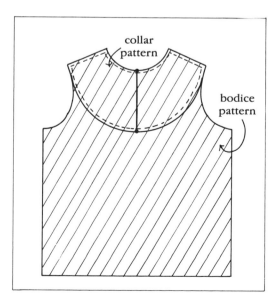

FIG. 2-23. For rounded bow collar, curve outside collar edge and extend to armscye.

■ COLLARS WITH CUT-OUTS

FIG. 2-24. Collars with cut-outs.

Shaped openings are cut from the upper collar to expose a contrast-fabric undercollar (Fig. 2-24). Choose an under collar fabric that is desirable on both sides because the wrong side will show through the cut-outs. For variety, weave an elongated scarf in and out of the collar openings.

■ PATTERN AND DESIGN CONSIDERATIONS

Begin with any collar pattern and make a template for the shape of the openings. Trace the template onto the pattern, repeating the shapes at regular intervals and positioning them at least 1″ apart. If desired, you can make the openings closer, but separate facing pieces must be used in Step 2.

For added interest, vary the angle of the shape as you repeat it, or vary the shape itself (Fig. 2-25). For collars that roll, position the shapes closer to the outside edge of the collar.

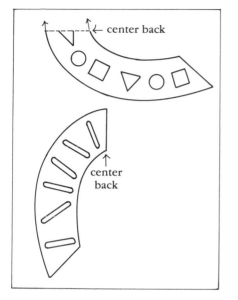

FIG. 2-25. For variety, vary angles of shapes or vary shapes themselves. Repeat chosen shapes at regular intervals.

■ CONSTRUCTION STEPS

1. Cut one upper collar from contrasting fabric and one under collar from fashion fabric. Cut a third collar from sheer fabric such as organza or organdy. The sheer collar is used to face the shapes. Transfer the shape markings from the pattern onto the sheer collar. If the cut-outs are less than 1″ apart, cut a separate facing piece for each cut-out.

2. Pin the sheer collar to the right side of the upper collar and stitch around the shape markings using a short stitch length (15–20 stitches per inch).

3. Cut the sheer facing apart between the shapes (Fig. 2-26). Cut the center of the

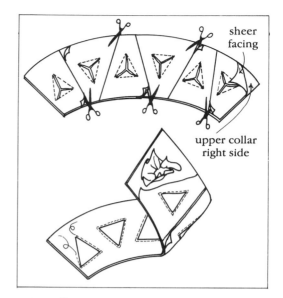

FIG. 2-26. Clip shear facing apart between shapes. Cut center of shapes clipping through both layers to corners. Turn sheer fabric to wrong side and edgestitch around openings.

shapes clipping through both layers and snipping to, but not through, the corner stitching on the shapes.

4. Turn the sheer fabric to the wrong side and press, rolling the seam to the wrong side so the facing doesn't show from the right side. Edge stitch around the shaped openings to hold the facing in place.

5. Stitch the outside edges of the upper and under collars right sides together. Trim the allowances as needed, turn the collar right side out and press. If you won't be threading a scarf through the cut outs, you may edgestitch again to tack the collars together at the cut outs. Complete the garment following the pattern guidesheet.

■ SHAWL COLLAR VARIATIONS

FIG. 2-27. Shawl collar variations: draped shawl and winged shawl.

Shawl-collar options are endless with only simple pattern modifications (Fig. 2-27).

■ PATTERN AND DESIGN CONSIDERATIONS

1. Choose a blouse or jacket pattern with a simple shawl collar. On a basic shawl collar pattern, the collar is connected to the garment front and extends past the shoulder (Fig. 2-28). When the garment is constructed, the extension attaches at the back of the neckline.

2. By varying the shape of the collar's outside edge, you can customize any shawl collar. Consider a scalloped design (Fig. 2-29) or create your own design using the Designers' Templates in the Appendix to experiment. To

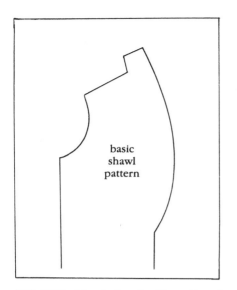

FIG. 2-28. A basic shawl collar pattern has collar connected to garment and extending past shoulder.

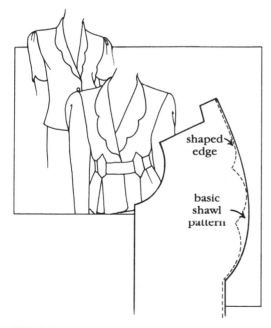

FIG. 2-29. For variety, change shape of collar's outside edge.

duplicate the winged or draped shawl options in Figure 2-27, copy the pattern in Figure 2-30.

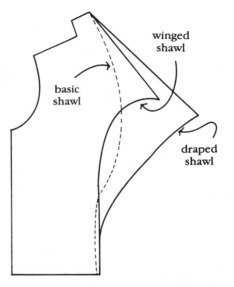

FIG. 2-30. Draw winged-shawl or draped-shawl patterns using a basic shawl pattern as a guide.

3. To widen a shawl, such as for a sailor collar, you'll need to adjust the collar extension. Cut four slashes to but not through the inside edge and spread each slash ½" (Fig. 2-31). Widen the collar and redraw the outside edge as desired.

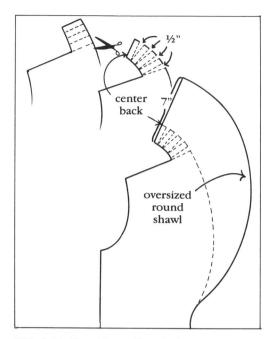

FIG. 2-31. To widen collar, slash and spread, then redraw outside edge.

4. Redraw the outside edge of the facing using the adjusted bodice pattern as a guide. Be sure to widen the facing to accommodate any width you may have added to the collar.

5. Construct the garment following the pattern guidesheet, using the newly shaped bodice and facing pieces.

ENDLESS OPTIONS
For a color-blocked shawl (Fig. 2-32), reshape the collar as desired and redraw the facing, following the instructions above. Cut the facing pattern apart, as shown. Add seam allowances to the newly cut edges. Cut the facing pieces from contrasting fabrics and seam them together. Insert piping into the seam for added variety.

For an elongated shawl (Fig. 2-32), extend the shawl collar to the hemline for a full-length collar. Be sure to extend the facing to accommodate the lengthened collar.

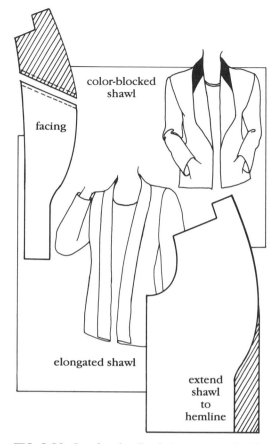

FIG. 2-32. Cut shawl-collar facing apart and add seam allowances for color-blocked shawl. Extend shawl to hemline for elongated shawl.

■ STITCHED-ON COLLAR

FIG. 2-33. Stitched-on collar.

This collar is constructed separately, then stitched to the outside of a completed garment (Fig. 2-33). The shape and size options are endless. Consider using contrasting color or print fabrics for the stitched-on collar and lapel pieces.

Before designing the collar and lapel pieces, construct the garment. If the garment is to be lined, attach the facing but wait to insert the lining until after the collar and lapel pieces are attached.

■ PATTERN AND DESIGN CONSIDERATIONS

1. Make paper collar and lapel cut-outs to determine the desired size and shape. These will serve as design templates so you can visualize the design ideas on *your* body. Use the center-front seamline of the bodice pattern as a guide to shape the center edge of the collar cut-outs. Consider some of the examples shown (Fig. 2-34).

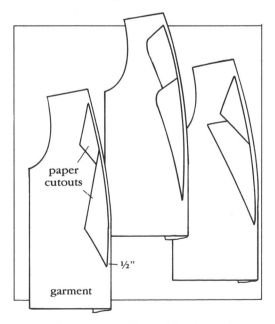

paper cutouts

½"

garment

FIG. 2-34. Pin paper collar and lapel templates to garment front to determine desired size and shape.

2. To visualize the finished collar and lapel, attach the cutouts to the garment (double-stick tape works well), positioning the center-front edge of the cut-outs approximately ½" from the front edge of the garment as the finished collar and lapel will be attached. Try on the garment in front of a full-length mirror. Readjust the length and outside edge of the cut outs and reposition them as desired, until satisfied with the look.

3. Add ¼" seam allowances to the outside edges of the collar and lapel cut-outs.

■ **CONSTRUCTION STEPS**

1. Cut four of each collar and lapel piece from fabric (two for each side of the garment).

2. Sew the upper and under collar pieces right sides together, stitching along the outside edges. Stop the stitching ¼" from the center-front edge and backstitch to secure (Fig. 2-35). Trim and clip the allowances, then

turn the collar pieces right side out. Press the pieces so the seamline rolls toward the under collar.

3. Turn the unstitched edge of the under collar ⅜" to the inside and the upper-collar edge ¼" to the inside. Press and blindstitch the edges so the seamline doesn't show on the upper collar side (Fig. 2-36).

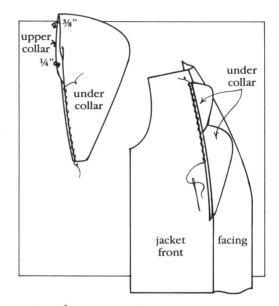

FIG. 2-36. Turn unstitched collar edges to inside and blindstitch. Handstitch collar pieces to garment front.

4. In this step, you'll be stitching the pieces to the garment with the upper collar toward the right side of the garment, then flipping the collars back onto the garment. Position the collar pieces onto the garment and hand stitch them in place, being careful not to catch the facing in the stitching. Fold the collars back onto the garment and press.

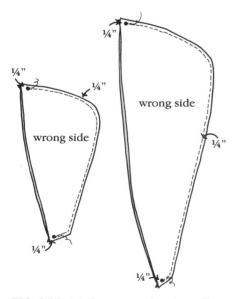

FIG. 2-35. Stitch upper and under collars and lapels together stopping ¼" from the inside edge.

OPEN-END, BIAS COLLAR

FIG. 2-37. Open-end, bias collar.

Replace any collar with this unique, bias-cut option, a quick and easy method for a tried-and-true perfect collar. This technique works well as a stand-up collar with a band, as well as the more traditional lay-down collar. Use soft, light-to medium-weight fabric for an ideal draped

roll. The collar ends are left open to accentuate the bias cut (Fig. 2-37).

PATTERN AND DESIGN CONSIDERATIONS

1. Use this technique to replace a collar on any blouse or dress pattern. To make the collar pattern, cut a rectangle the collar length (the length of the garment neckline) plus 3″ (1½″ will be folded under at each end). Cut the width two times the desired finished collar width plus two seam allowances. Exaggerate the width for a dramatic effect.
2. Mark foldlines 1½″ from each end. Mark the shoulder line on the collar pattern. Fold the ends back along the foldline, then fold the pattern in half lengthwise. Taper the neckline edges beginning at the shoulder marking and tapering up to ½″ at the folded end (Fig. 2-38). Mark a bias grainline 45 degrees from

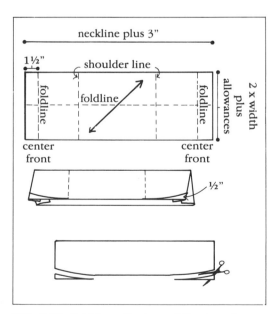

FIG. 2-38. Cut bias collar to neckline length plus 3″. Fold ends to inside. Trim ½″ off lower edges, beginning at folded front and tapering toward shoulder lines.

DESIGN & SEW TIP

Marking a Bias Grainline

Mark the lengthwise grain on the pattern by drawing a vertical arrow. (There's no need to redraw the lengthwise grainline if using a pattern that already has it marked.) Mark the crosswise grain with a horizontal arrow at a right angle to the lengthwise grainline. Measure a line halfway between the

lengthwise and crosswise arrows and mark this diagonal line as the true bias grainline. To easily measure the halfway point, fold the pattern so the lengthwise and crosswise grains meet, causing a fold mark to be positioned evenly between the two grainlines (Fig. 2-39).

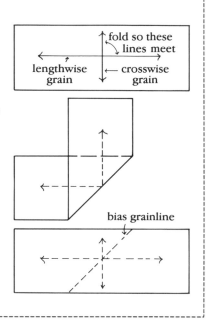

FIG. 2-39. To mark bias grainline, first mark lengthwise and crosswise grains on pattern. Fold pattern diagonally so lengthwise and crosswise grains meet. Foldline indicates the true bias grainline.

the center foldline. (For information on marking a bias grainline, refer to the above Design and Sew Tip.

■ **CONSTRUCTION STEPS**

1. Cut one collar on the bias grainline. Fold the ends to the wrong side along the foldlines.
2. Fold the collar in half lengthwise, wrong sides together, and baste the neckline edges together (Fig. 2-40).
3. Attach the collar to the garment following the pattern guidesheet and matching the center-front and shoulder markings with the center-front and shoulder seams of the garment.

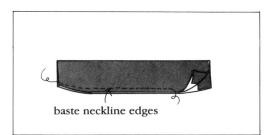

baste neckline edges

FIG. 2-40. Baste raw edges together leaving folded ends unstitched.

■ COLLAR DETAILS

FIG. 2-41. Add collar details for personalized style. A wide collar ruffle, ribbon trim, loops from narrow tubing, soutache couching, and narrow pleats with decorative stitching are just a few options.

Consider the following collar details and embellishments to give any collar personalized style (Fig. 2-41):

Wide ruffle inset into outside collar seam.

Ribbon or lace trim, or decorative stitching adds a simple but unique touch.

Inset tubing to make loops along outside edge.

Soutache trim or narrow tubing makes upper-collar couching.

Pre-pleated upper collar embellished with decorative stitching.

Contrast fabric and trim stitched to upper collar and embellished with a tassel. (See color section.)

CHAPTER 3

NOVELTY NECKLINES

The neckline is a basic but essential design line on many garments. A neckline can be accentuated with a unique shape or a special embellishment. Or you may prefer a more conventional shape that is particularly suitable for your face shape and figure type. This chapter concentrates on the design considerations in choosing a neckline shape, as well as the more practical aspects of adjusting the pattern to reshape the neckline. Many of the collar techniques in the previous chapter can be enhanced by reshaping the neckline before marking the collar pattern.

■ RESHAPING THE NECKLINE

Reshape any neckline for an easy-to-make, yet custom design. Duplicate the conventional shapes in Figure 3-1, choose one of the novelty shapes in Figure 3-4, or draft your own design.

✂ N O T E : Throughout the book, we often refer to "a basic jewel neckline." This is a plain round neckline at the base of the throat. This simple, plain line acts as a good starting place for designing other more flattering necklines.

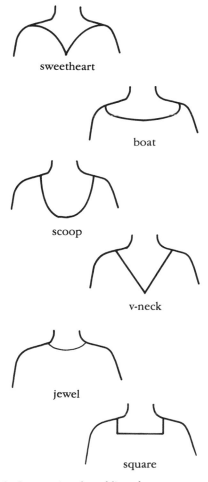

FIG. 3-1. Conventional neckline shapes.

■ DESIGN CONSIDERATIONS

When determining the general design line and fine-tuning the shape, consider the following:

Accentuate Your Face Shape—Necklines that repeat the face shape are often the most flattering. Is your face shape oval, round, square, heart-shaped or diamond-shaped. To determine your shape, pull your hair away from your face and stand in front of the mirror. Look straight on, or ask a friend for an objective opinion. Many consider the oval shape the most pleasing. Experiment with conventional neckline shapes that give the illusion of an oval-shaped face.

Create Balance—Consider your figure and keep in mind that horizontal lines create a broader appearance while vertical lines give a narrower and longer look. Use this idea to help balance your figure or accentuate a positive feature. For example, use a deep scoop or V neckline to lengthen a short neck, narrow broad shoulders, or accentuate a long shapely neck. Consider a wide boat-neck or wide square necklines to shorten a long neck, broaden narrow shoulders, or balance a wide hipline.

Combining Factors—There may be combining factors that make balance and line decisions difficult. This calls for a creative combination. For example, suppose you have a short neck and narrow shoulders. A narrow V or scoop neckline balances the neck, but isn't the best design for your narrow shoulders. Consider horizontal top-stitching or a yoke to widen the shoulders. Here are some ideas for creative camouflaging:

- Inset sleeves, a dropped waistline, or a belt at the hip will either narrow or balance wide shoulders.
- Shoulder pads, horizontal stitching, wide collars and lapels, or off-center jewelry and scarves are unique ways to add width to narrow shoulders.

■ Scarves and fancy broaches are ideal ways to draw the eye upward to accentuate an oval face shape or balance large hips.

✂ N O T E : We prefer to weigh the above figure-flattering ideas lightly in the design process. It's important not to get bogged down in this phase of design or the creative process may be diminished. In the overall fashion scheme, the garment you adore the most is going to be the one you wear the most.

Determining the Best Shape for You—Here are some ideas on how to choose basic neckline shapes that look the best on your figure. Try this technique with a plain, solid-colored bodice that has a high-neckline. (Consider making a basic muslin bodice; it's easy to do and comes in handy when designing details such as

FIG. 3-2. Use drapery beads or textured cord to experiment with different neckline shapes.

this one.) Try on the garment or basic bodice and stand in front of a full-length mirror (an essential item for every sewing room). You'll need a string of drapery beads or textured cord. Drapery beads work best and can be found at most fabric stores. Hang the strand around your neck and move them around to create different neckline shapes (Fig. 3-2). The beads will cling to the garment fabric, making it easy to shape. Experiment until you find the best shape for your face, shoulders, bustline, and hair.

■ **PATTERN CONSIDERATIONS**

1. When you've decided on a desired shape, mark the bodice with a soluble marker. Remove the bodice, and true up the line to create a smooth and evenly shaped curve. If the neckline is symmetrical, only true up the mark on one side of the garment. For an asymmetrical neckline, you must mark both sides.

2. Transfer the neckline marking to the front and back pattern pieces, then add a seam allowance. If transferring the marking to both the left and right sides of the pattern, be sure both halves are exactly the same (unless you're making an asymmetrical neckline). When adjusting the patterns, be sure the shoulder seems on the front and back bodice pieces are the same length.

✂ N O T E : If making a low scoop or V neckline, the pattern should be adjusted to eliminate gaping. See "Resolving a Gaping Neckline" beginning on page 39.

3. If the pattern calls for a neckline facing, make front and back facing patterns. See the Design and Sew Tip below.

4. Construct the garment following the pattern guidesheet, using the updated bodice and facing patterns.

✂ N O T E : This procedure can also be used to reshape the neckline of a garment with a center-front closure, such as a collarless jacket.

Drafting A Facing Pattern

Trace the shoulder, neckline, and center front seamlines and cutting lines from the newly adjusted bodice front (Fig. 3-3). Draw the outside edge of the facing 2½″ from the neck seamline. Transfer the notches or other matchpoints to the facing pattern. Repeat this procedure for the back facing, tracing the shoulder, neckline, and center-back lines from the back bodice.

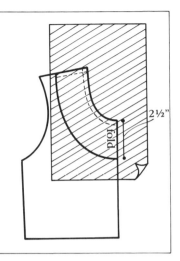

FIG. 3-3. Trace shoulder, neckline, and center front. Draw outside line 2½″ from neckline.

ENDLESS OPTIONS

In addition to the conventional shapes shown in Figure 3-1, there are endless options for novelty shapes (Fig. 3-4). Use the Designers' Templates in the Appendix to generate ideas for your own neckline designs.

■ RESOLVING A GAPING NECKLINE

Natural body curves such as the bust or shoulder blades may cause the bias portion of a large neckline opening to gape or pull away from the

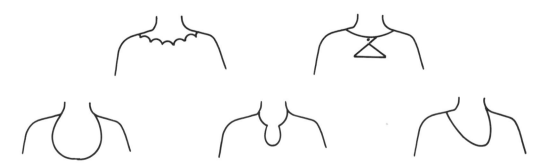

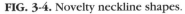
FIG. 3-4. Novelty neckline shapes.

body. When reshaping a neckline, a low scoop or "V" must be adjusted to fit close to the body. As you design new, scooping necklines, use these adjustments for an ideal, custom fit.

■ PATTERN AND DESIGN CONSIDERATIONS

The adjustments for resolving a gaping neckline vary for the front and back necklines, so procedures are listed separately.

✄ N O T E : Although the front and back necklines can both be reshaped, they cannot both be lowered and still retain ideal neckline fit.

FRONT ADJUSTMENTS

1. Hold the pattern up to your body and mark the bust point. This will be used as a pivot point when reducing fullness in the neckline.
2. Slash the pattern from the lower portion of the neckline to, but not through, the bust point. Slash the pattern again from the waist up to, but not through, the bust point (Fig. 3-5).

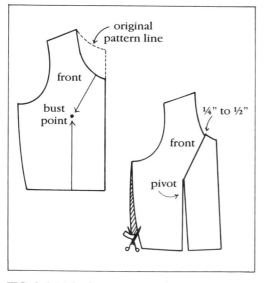

FIG. 3-5. Make front pattern adjustments to eliminate a gaping neckline.

3. Pivot the pattern so the neckline slash overlaps ¼″ to ½″. (Spread more for a deeper neckline or fuller bustline.) The waistline slash will open the same amount as the overlap.
4. The added waist fullness can be incorporated into the garment or trimmed off at the side seam for a fitted waistline, as shown in Figure 3-5.

BACK ADJUSTMENTS

1. Have a friend hold the pattern up to your back and mark the approximate location of where the shoulder blade protrudes. Because the shoulder blade may cause gaping, it acts like the bust point for the back adjustment. This will be the pivot point. Lay the pattern on a flat surface and mark a slash line from the center of the neckline to, but not through, the pivot point. Mark another slash line from the waist up to the pivot point (Fig. 3-6).

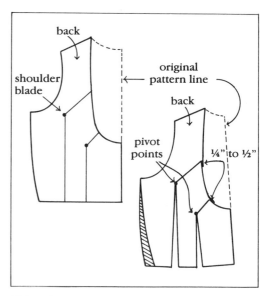

FIG. 3-6. Make back pattern adjustments to eliminate a gaping neckline.

2. If the neckline is particularly low, such as two-thirds to the waist, you will need to make an additional adjustment. Mark a slash line from the lower portion of the neckline in the bias direction toward the center of the bodice. The end of this line will be the pivot point. Mark another slash line from the waist up to the pivot point.

3. Cut the pattern along the slash lines to, but not through, the pivot points. Pivot the pattern so the neckline slashes overlap ¼" to ½". (Overlap more for a deeper neckline.) Spread the waistline slashes the same amount as the overlaps.

4. The added waist fullness can be incorporated into the garment or trimmed off at the side seam for a fitted waistline.

ENDLESS OPTIONS

The following construction techniques can also be used to control gaping on either the front or back necklines. For each of the following techniques, mark a 3" area with the most *bias* on each side of the neckline.

■ Cut 2½" of clear elastic. Stitch the elastic in the seam allowance, stretching it to fit the 3" portion of the neckline you marked.

■ Stitch two or three rows of short gathering stitches in the 3" portions of the neckline seam allowance. Pull up the threads just slightly to reduce the fullness in the neckline. Steam-shrink out the fullness from the seam allowances.

■ Cut a 2½" length of stay tape or seam binding. Stitch the tape to the garment seamline, stretching the tape to fit the 3" portion of the neckline and finger-easing the garment to fit the tape.

■ Fuse a narrow strip of fusible interfacing in the biased portion of the neckline to help retain the neckline shape.

■ NOVELTY NOTCHED NECKLINE

FIG. 3-7. Novelty notched neckline.

Adjust the neckline shapes of collarless projects to create the look of a notched-collar. This technique is ideal for button-front blazers or blouses. Begin with a collarless pattern or eliminate the collar, then reshape the neckline to create unique notches as shown (Fig. 3-7).

For ideal notch placement and size, cut half the bodice front from muslin and draw the notched neckline before cutting your garment fabric. Follow the Pattern Considerations for reshaping the neckline, beginning on page 38. Redraw the facing to match the newly adjusted neckline (see Design and Sew Tip on page 39, *Drafting a Facing Pattern*). To accentuate the shape, bind the edge as done for the center design in Figure 3-7.

■ DOUBLE NECKLINE

FIG. 3-8. Double neckline.

The bodice is made with two layers, creating two necklines varied in size and shape. Our favorite double neckline has an opaque underlayer with a simple jewel neckline and a sheer outer layer with a larger asymmetrical neckline (Fig. 3-8).

■ PATTERN AND DESIGN CONSIDERATIONS

Use a pullover blouse pattern with a simple neckline and no collar. Make a duplicate of the front and back bodice pieces. Mark one copy for the under layer and one for the outer layer. Adjust the necklines so the outer layer has a larger neckline than the under layer. For variety, we made the outer layer asymmetrical as shown in Figure 3-8.

■ CONSTRUCTION STEPS

1. Cut the bodice patterns from two fabric types, one for the under layer and one for the outer layer. Cut the outer layer $\frac{1}{8}''$ to $\frac{1}{4}''$ larger on all edges.

2. Position the layers together with the right side of the under layer to the wrong side of the outer layer. Try on the blouse and adjust the necklines so the outer layer is larger than the under layer. The outer neckline should drop about 2″ to 3″ lower in the front. Alter the shape as desired. Be sure the smaller neckline is large enough to fit over your head.

3. Bind both necklines with matching or contrasting bias-cut binding. Cut 1″-wide bias strips and finish one long edge. Seam the short ends to fit the neckline. Stitch the right side of the binding to the right side of the neckline with a $\frac{1}{4}''$ seam allowance. Wrap the binding over the allowances and stitch-in-the-ditch from the right side (Fig. 3-9).

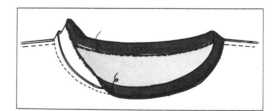

FIG. 3-9. Stitch binding to neckline right sides together with $\frac{1}{4}''$ seam allowance. Wrap binding to wrong side and stitch-in-the-ditch.

4. For a cap-sleeve or sleeveless blouse, finish the sleeve edges separately. Tack the layers together at the shoulder seam.

5. For a blouse with separate sleeves, baste the armscye edges together and attach the sleeves to both layers following your pattern guidesheet.

✂ N O T E : Consider using this technique on a blouse with a zipper or faced closure. Follow the instructions above, binding only the outside layer. Construct the closure, treating both layers as one, then bind the inside neckline.

■ WOVEN-TUBE NECKLINE

FIG. 3-10. Woven-tube neckline.

Fabric tubes create a beautiful focal point for this simple V-shaped neckline (Fig. 3-10). Choose a blouse pattern with a basic jewel neckline and a back closure, or a pullover blouse with no closure. Use soft, pliable fabric for the tubes such as silks or silkies, very soft cotton, or rayons.

■ CONSTRUCTION STEPS

1. Cut out the blouse and stitch the shoulder seams, following the pattern guidesheet.
2. Try on the blouse to determine the desired depth of the neckline. Use an erasable marker and redraw the neckline with a V front. Make the neckline lower in front than usual because the woven tubes will fill in about 2″ to 4″ of the V.
3. Trim the neckline to the cutting line making sure the right and left sides are identical. No need to allow for seam allowances here because the neckline will be bound. Staystitch the V portion of the neckline, stitching 2″ up each side of the V and ¼″ from the edge.
4. Bind the neckline edge with bias binding or decorative trim. Binding made from the same fabric as the tubes is our favorite finish.
5. Make six to eight 10″ tubes with a ¼″ to ½″ finished width. Follow the Design and Sew Tip below for *Easy Fabric Tubes*.

DESIGN & SEW TIP

Easy Fabric Tubes

Cut fabric strips two times the desired width plus ½″ for seam allowances. A bias grain is preferable if you will be curving the tubes, such as for the woven-tube neckline, couching, or loops, otherwise a straight grain will work fine. There are a number of methods for stitching and turning tubes. Here are two of our favorites:

Stitch-and-Turn—Stitch the tube right sides together with a ¼″ seam (or less for narrower tubes). Turn the tube right side out using a loop turner, Fasturn, or bodkin. These tools can usually be found at your local fabric store, but if they can't, snip a small hole ¾″ from the end of the tube and turn it with a bobby pin (Fig. 3-11).

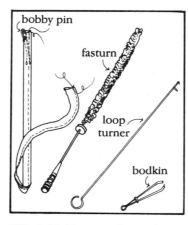

FIG. 3-11. Turn spaghetti tubes right side out using bobby pin, Fasturn, loop turner, or bodkin.

Simply Serged Tubes—If you have a serger, try this: Serge a thread chain 3″ longer than the tube and do not cut the chain from the machine. Wrap the fabric around the chain with the right sides together and position the chain just inside the fold of the fabric strip (Fig. 3-12). Serge-seam the long edges of the strip, being careful not to catch the chain in the stitching. Gently pull the thread chain to turn the tube right side out.

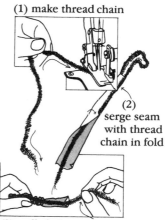

(1) make thread chain

(2) serge seam with thread chain in fold

(3) pull chain to turn

FIG. 3-12. Turn spaghetti tubes right side out using a serger thread chain.

6. Press the tubes so the seam is to the underside. As you press, gently pull the outside edge of the tube with your hand and use the iron to mold a slight curve in the tube, stretching one edge and shrinking the other (Fig. 3-13).
7. Trace the V shape of the neckline onto water-soluble or tear-away stabilizer (plain paper will also work), using the stitching line of the binding as a guide. Repeat the marking on the wrong side of the stabilizer as

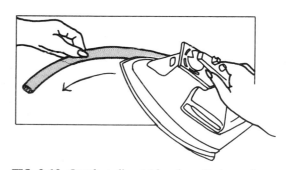

FIG. 3-13. Gently pull outside edge of tube and use iron to mold curve.

well. Measure and mark points A, B, and C on the stabilizer, as shown (Fig. 3-14).

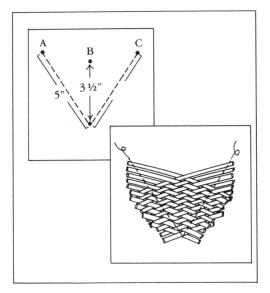

FIG. 3-14. Draw V shape of neckline onto stabilizer, then weave tubes onto the V, pinning each tube in place. Stitch tubes to stabilizer.

8. Lay the stabilizer onto a flat surface and position the tubes on top of the stabilizer. Pin the tubes close together in one direction so the ends curve downward. Pin and trim the tubes one-at-a-time, allowing the ends to extend 1″ beyond the neckline markings. Weave additional tubes in the opposite direction, pinning each tube as you go. (You will need to remove the original pins and repin as you weave.)
9. Turn the stabilizer over and stitch the tubes along the stitching line, following the marking on the wrong side of the stabilizer.
10. Remove the stabilizer. Position the right side of the woven tubes to the wrong side of the neckline, lining up the stitching lines. Stitch-in-the-ditch of the neckline binding to secure the tubes.

11. Trim the ends of the tubes and finish the raw edges with serging, binding, or an overcast stitch; or enclose the ends with a fitted facing. If desired, sew a neckline facing to enclose the raw edges.

ENDLESS OPTIONS
Use this eye-catching detail to accent any garment edge, such as the bottom of sleeves, shirttails, pant legs, or overlays.

■ SCARF-EMBELLISHED NECKLINE

FIG. 3-15. Scarf-embellished neckline and grommet/chain variation.

This accessorized neckline draws the eye upward and gracefully frames the face. A V neckline is our favorite shape for this technique; however, round and oval necklines also work well. Construct this neckline with buttonholes and a scarf, or for an eye-catching variation, use grommets and a lightweight chain (Fig. 3-15).

■ PATTERN AND DESIGN CONSIDERATIONS

Begin with a blouse or dress pattern and adjust the neckline shape as desired, following the instructions for "Reshaping the Neckline" on page 37. Redraw the facing pattern to fit the newly shaped neckline. Make the facing 3″ wide to support the buttonholes. If you'll be adjusting the buttonhole length or position, be sure the facing is wide enough to incorporate them.

■ CONSTRUCTION STEPS

1. Fuse medium-weight interfacing to the wrong sides of the facing pieces. Join the front and back facings at the shoulder seams. Serge- or zigzag-finish the outside edge of the facing.
2. Sew the front and back bodices together at the shoulder seams. Stitch the facing to the neckline with the right sides together.
3. Carefully measure and mark the buttonhole placement (Fig. 3-16). Mark for 1″ to 1½″ buttonholes, depending on the thickness of the scarf you'll be using. Position the buttonholes perpendicular to and 1″ away from the neckline. Mark them in sets of two with 1″ between the two, and space the sets 2½″ to 4″ apart. Refer to Design and Sew Tip on page 49, *Nearly Perfect Buttonholes.*

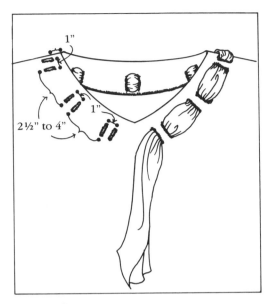

FIG. 3-16. Mark neckline for buttonholes. Stitch buttonholes through garment and facing.

4. Sew the buttonholes as marked, stitching through both the bodice and facing layers. Complete the garment following the pattern guidesheet. Weave a complementary oblong scarf or ribbon through the buttonholes. Make the scarf long enough to go through the buttonholes and around the neck, leaving plenty of length to tie and hang down in the front.

ENDLESS OPTIONS

■ Use grommets instead of buttonholes and weave a lightweight chain in and out of the grommets (see Fig. 3-15). Fuse interfacing to the neckline area of the garment to support the grommets. Attach the grommets before attaching the facing; the grommets will not be attached to the facing.

■ Construct faced slits instead of large buttonholes. Fuse interfacing to the neckline area of the garment to support the slits. Create the slits before attaching the facing. (a) Mark the

slit positions and place a sheer fabric patch (silk organza) on the right side of the garment over each marked slit (Fig. 3-17).

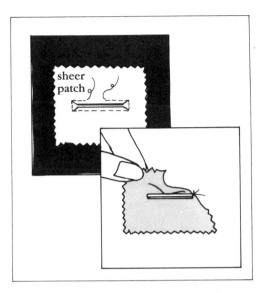

FIG. 3-17. For faced slits, place sheer-fabric patch to right side of garment. Stitch around slit marking, cut through center, and turn to wrong side (bottom illustration).

✄ NOTE: If desired, face the slits with fusible interfacing instead of sheer fabric, as explained for the slit used in the "Cross-Front Closure" on page 127.
(b) Use a short stitch (15–20 stitches per inch) and sew through the garment and organza, guiding the needle around the slit making two short stitches at each end. (c) Cut through the center of the stitching, turn the organza to the wrong side, and press.

■ If you prefer not to face the neckline, bind the neckline edge instead. Interface the neckline area of the garment to provide support for the buttonholes, slits, or grommets.

■ Make buttonholes in the front of the garment only, then attach the scarf in the shoulder seam. This is ideal for a blouse or dress with a back zipper closure.

DESIGN & SEW TIP

Nearly Perfect Buttonholes

The buttonholes are particularly visible when repeated around the neckline. Here are tips for better buttonholes:

Always make a sample buttonhole, stitching through the fabric, interfacing, and facing, exactly as you would on the garment. Repeat the testing until the buttonhole is just as you want it for the garment.

Stitch one to three times around the buttonhole, depending on what's needed to keep its edges from fraying.

For delicate fabrics, use machine embroidery thread to create a fine buttonhole without heavy thread buildup.

Before cutting open the buttonhole, turn to the wrong side of the buttonhole and dab the center with fray retardant.

After cutting the buttonhole, trim any loose threads from the center and coat the edges again with fray retardant. Work from the wrong side and blot any excess with a paper towel. Allow the buttonhole to dry, then press. Repeat the process if necessary until the buttonholes are ravel-free.

If the interfacing shows on the inside of the buttonhole, use a matching permanent marker to camouflage the interfacing.

After stitching and cutting large buttonholes, stitch them again to enclose the inside cut edge. Pull the buttonhole open slightly and use a wide zigzag stitch so the needle swings over the cut edge to the inside of the buttonhole.

If the fabric does not allow for a suitable buttonhole because of weight, texture, or thickness, consider a faced slit (explained under Endless Options on page 48).

CHAPTER 4

SAVVY SLEEVES

Experimenting with sleeve design is one of our favorite designing options. The sleeve is a rather small section of the garment, but allows a tremendous number of wearable options. By simply changing the sleeve on a basic blouse or dress pattern, you can create enough garment variations for a unique and stylish wardrobe. Sleeve design can be varied by adding seams, trims, tucks, pleats, buttons, ruffles, and much more, all done with simple pattern alterations. We've included a few variations in this chapter and encourage you to use these as a springboard in creating additional sleeve designs.

BUTTON-DOWN, FLARED SLEEVE

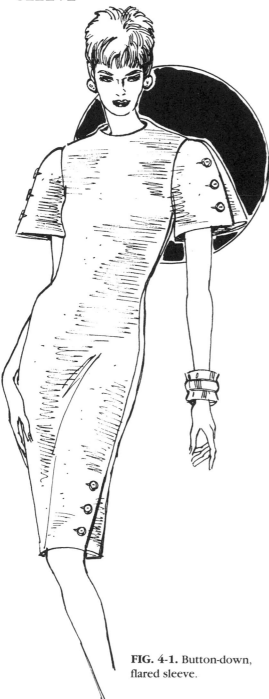

This charming short sleeve is cut with a slight amount of flare and is embellished with a buttoned overlap, a stylish adaptation from a high-quality ready-to-wear garment. The added flare is subtle, but gives the sleeve its unique and marvelous styling (Fig. 4-1).

We prefer lightweight to mediumweight fabric for this sleeve because it is constructed in two layers. However, heavyweight fabric works well when backed with a lightweight lining (see the notes in the following steps for using a separate lining).

■ PATTERN AND DESIGN CONSIDERATIONS

1. Use a basic straight-sleeve pattern with a fitted cap. Trace the stitching lines (not the cutting lines) onto pattern paper, stopping the underarm seam 3½″ below the armscye seamline. Transfer all the markings, including the notches and grainline.
2. Mark the sleeve center by drawing a line down the center of the sleeve pattern, parallel to the grainline. Cut the pattern apart on the center line.
3. Add a 1⅝″-wide extension to the center cut edge on both sides of the pattern. This edge will be cut on the fabric fold (Fig. 4-2).

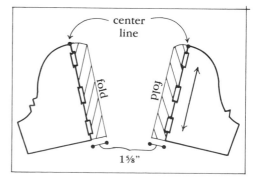

FIG. 4-2. Cut sleeve pattern apart on center line. Add 1⅝″-wide extension to center edges. Center edges will be cut on the fold.

FIG. 4-1. Button-down, flared sleeve.

✄ N O T E : If backing the sleeve with lining fabric, add an additional ⅝″ (seam allowance) to the extension for a total extension width of 2¼″.

4. To add flare, slash each pattern piece four times, cutting from the lower edge to (but not through) the top of the cap. Space the slashes evenly between the sleeve center line and the underarm seam (Fig. 4-3). (See the Design and Sew Tip on page 54. *Slash and Spread for Fullness or Flare.*)

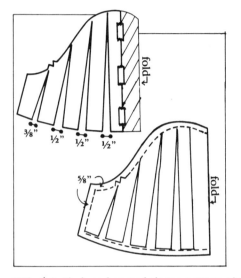

FIG. 4-3. Slash and spread sleeve pattern pieces to add flare. Add seam allowances to all edges except the foldline.

5. Spread each slash ½″. Because the underarm area requires less flare, spread the slash below the notches a scant ⅜″. True up the lines and add ⅝″ seam allowances to all edges except the foldline.

■ CONSTRUCTION STEPS

1. Cut one front and one back for each sleeve, positioning the extension edges on the fold.

Transfer the notches and center line markings to the fabric with a disappearing marker.

✄ N O T E : If using lining fabric, cut one front and back of fashion fabric and one front and back of lining fabric. Seam the lining to the fashion fabric right sides together along the extension edges.

2. Fold each sleeve section right sides together and seam the lower edge (Fig. 4-4). Trim the allowances at the corners; then turn the pieces right side out and press.

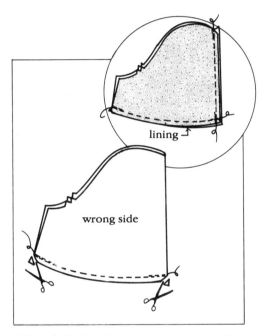

FIG. 4-4. Fold each sleeve section right sides together and seam the lower edges. Trim, then turn right side out.

3. Position the front and back right sides together at the underarm seam (Fig. 4-5). You'll need to open out the sleeves and pull the underarm seam flat for stitching.

4. Press the allowances open, then place the wrong sides together and press the sleeve

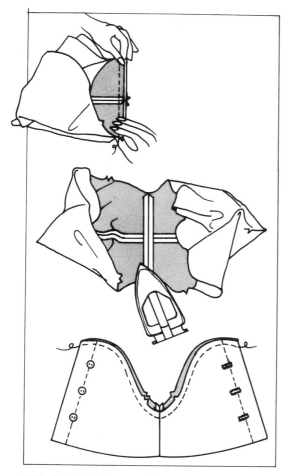

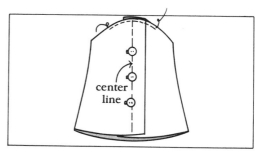

FIG. 4-6. Button the sleeve lapping front over back, aligning the center lines. Baste overlapped layers at upper edge.

4-5. Attach the buttons and construct the buttonholes.

6. Button the sleeve, lapping the front over the back and aligning the center marks. Baste the overlapped layers together at the upper edge (Fig. 4-6).

7. Repeat Steps 2 through 6 for the remaining sleeve. (When marking the buttons and buttonholes in Step 5, be sure to make the sleeves opposite each other so you'll have one right and one left sleeve.) Construct the garment and attach the sleeves following the pattern guidesheet.

FIG. 4-5. Stitch front and back, right sides together, at underarm seam. Press seams open, then press sleeve flat. Place wrong sides together matching upper raw edges. Baste raw edges together. Mark and sew buttons and buttonholes.

flat. Baste the raw edges together along the armscye seam.

5. Mark the button and buttonhole placement, positioning the buttons on the center line of the back and the buttonholes ⅛″ over the center line of the front, as shown in Figure

DESIGN & SEW TIP

Slash and Spread for Fullness or Flare

Throughout this book, you are often requested to add fullness to a pattern using the slash-and-spread method. Here are some tips and guidelines to consider:

Before adding fullness or flare, we recommend that you remove the seam allowances. To keep your original pattern intact, trace the seamlines of the original, then make adjustments on the traced copy.

The slash-and-spread technique increases the amount of fabric in the area where you spread the pattern apart. Keeping this in mind, you can control where your fullness is by where you position the slash lines and how much you spread. For example, suppose you want more fullness at the center of the sleeve and less fullness in the underarm area. Spread the underarm slashes less than the slashes at the center of the sleeve, or make more slash marks at the sleeve center than at the underarm (see Figure 4-3).

Draw the slash lines parallel to the grainline shown on the pattern.

There are three types of fullness (Fig. 4-7):

Gathered/Even Fullness—Slash the pattern all the way through from top to bottom, then spread each section apart an equal amount. The slashed edges are parallel, to one another with equal spacing between the upper and lower portions. Because fullness is added to the upper seamline, the extra fabric must be compensated for when joining it to the garment, such as with gathers or pleats.

Flared Fullness—Slash just to the edge of the pattern, but don't cut all the way through. Spread the slashes apart. Because the slashes don't go all the way through the pattern, the slashes will only spread partially. The pattern makes a curved shape so that the lower part

is flared. The upper seamline remains the same length so there's no need to compensate with gathers or pleats.

Gathered with Flared Hem—The two types of fullness explained above can be combined to create fullness added to the upper seamline, as well as flare to the lower portion. Slash the pattern all the way through, then spread it apart more in the lower area than the upper area.

When spreading the pattern, arrange it over pattern drafting paper so the edges are in alignment. When the slashes are measured and positioned properly, tape the pattern in place to the drafting paper.

After you tape the pattern into position, carefully true up the edges; then add seam allowances. Use a curved ruler if desired.

Additional fabric may be required when using the slash and spread technique to add fullness or flare to a pattern.

Slash and Spread for Fullness or Flare *Continued*

slash-and-spread techniques

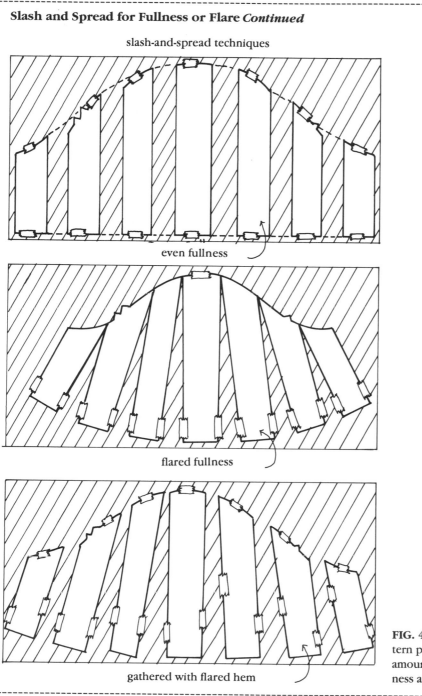

even fullness

flared fullness

gathered with flared hem

FIG. 4-7. Slash and spread pattern pieces in even or uneven amounts to achieve desired fullness and flare.

ENDLESS OPTIONS (FIG. 4-8)

■ Substitute a loop and button closure. Construct the sleeve following the lining technique and insert the loops in the seam.

■ If you're using lighter-weight fabric, consider adding additional flare for more of a draped sleeve.

■ Construct a different version of the button-down sleeve by eliminating the flare, an ideal look for a basic T-shirt. Follow Steps 1 through 3 of the Pattern and Design Considerations, then complete the Construction Steps.

■ Contrasting-color, bound or shaped button-holes add a unique variation.

FIG. 4-8. Consider these variations to the button down sleeve: (1) additional flare for lighter weight fabric sleeves with a looped and buttoned closure (2) more fitted T-shirt style sleeves that button down for casual interest, or (3) contrast-color triangular shaped buttonholes to create geometric variety.

Plate 1.
Stylish bodice overlays inspire flattering new looks for these traditional garment silhouettes. The back overlay (*left*) flatters the figure with its below-the-hip length and unique button-back shaping. Contrast cuffs and button epaulets complete the look. The complementary-color, sheer front overlay (*right*) adds soft feminine focus with multiple gathers into the shoulder seam and a large full bow which ties at the front. Both easy overlay additions are simply sewn into the garments' shoulder and side seams, hanging free at the armscyes

Plate 2.
The apron-front pant overlay (*left*) is shaped to a point in the front and ties with a large dramatic bow in the back. Oval window pockets with small button tabs add subtle variation. The flared skirt overlay (*right*) fits beautifully over a long straight skirt. The circular flare allows for a fitted waistline with flattering fullness at the bottom. Both overlays can be stitched to the garment at the waistline seam or, for versatility, made separate to be tied or buttoned onto the outside of the garment.

Plate 3.
Pleasing shapes at jacket-front edges create unique possibilities for exciting closures. The long fitted jacket (*left*) has a combination button/tie closure, while the jacket on the right has a shaped closure combined with a shaped tab to complete the waist-cinching style. For information on reshaping the edges, please refer to Chapter 6.

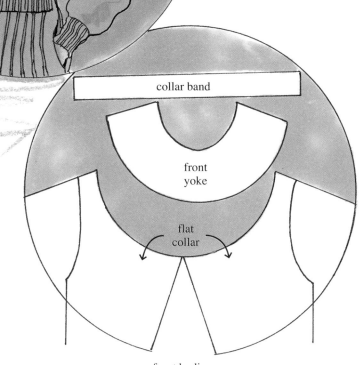

Plate 4.
Combined neckline and collar techniques are used to create the soft romance of this luxurious lace collection. To duplicate, cut a yoke from the bodice pattern. Draw a flat collar pattern shaped to fit the yoke line and cut wide enough to drape over the shoulders (for collar shaping, refer to Chapter 2). Cut a mandarin collar pattern the desired width by the measurement of the neckline seam. Add a back closure such as a keyhole opening or button overlap. Show off your favorite lace by trimming the edges and seamlines.

collar band

front
yoke

flat
collar

front bodice

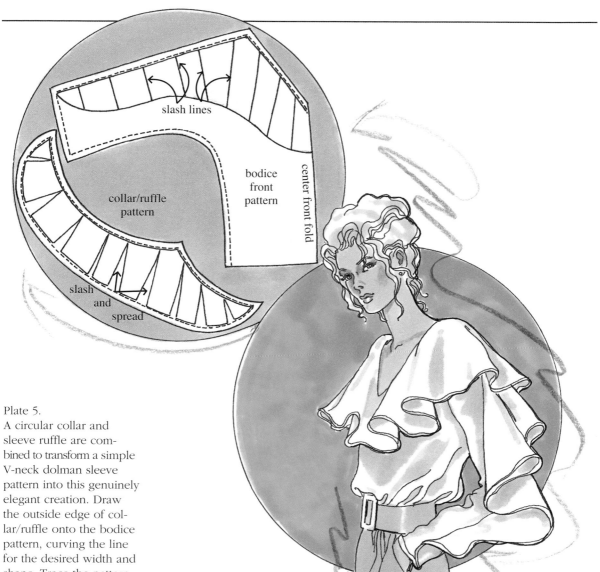

slash lines

collar/ruffle
pattern

bodice
front
pattern

center front fold

slash
and
spread

Plate 5.
A circular collar and
sleeve ruffle are com-
bined to transform a simple
V-neck dolman sleeve
pattern into this genuinely
elegant creation. Draw
the outside edge of col-
lar/ruffle onto the bodice
pattern, curving the line
for the desired width and
shape. Trace the pattern;
then slash and spread for
circular flare. Add seam
and hem allowances.

Plate 6.
Collar details create an ideal update for almost any fashion classic. Multiple collars trimmed with delicate lace (*left*) fashion this lovely blouse with sweet femininity. Create triple collars from the same collar pattern by staggering the widths. Color and texture variation frame the face of this two-toned trimmed collar (*right*). A contrasting piece of fabric is layered over the collar and trimmed with an elegant braid and tassel. The same detail is repeated on the bodice front with triple buttons for additional accent.

Plate 7.
Tiny buttonholes embell-
ish the entire edge of this
smart bolero jacket (*left*)
with six ball buttons along
the center front for functional fastening and a row
up each sleeve for savvy
repetition. The sassy
sweetheart inset (*right*) is
sure to invite attention to
the low scooping neckline
of this sporty knit.

Plate 8.
Beautiful button-on sleeves edged with lavish binding dramatize this simple sleeveless dress, a unique variation of the kimono-style sleeves shown in Chapter 4. To make the sleeves, use a basic set-in sleeve pattern and lower the armscye for ease of movement. Incorporate loops into the bound edge of the sleeve cap and sew corresponding buttons to the dress at the top of the armscye.

■ CENTER-SEAM DETAILING

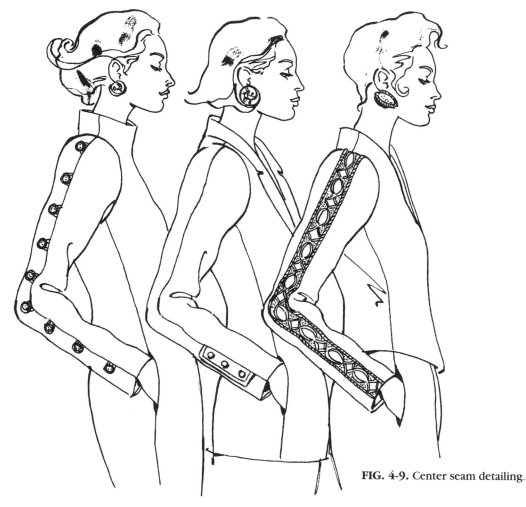

FIG. 4-9. Center seam detailing.

By adding a seam down the center of a sleeve, you open up a multitude of detail possibilities. A few of our favorites are shown in Figure 4-9, but you might have more fun designing your own options.

■ PATTERN CONSIDERATIONS

1. Use a basic sleeve pattern with a fitted cap and adjust the length as usual for your arm.
2. To mark the sleeve center, draw a vertical line from the center cap marking down the sleeve parallel to the grainline. Cut out the pattern, slashing it apart all the way through at the center line.
3. Add seam allowances to both center edges.
4. The center sleeve seam provides unique embellishment options. Consider loops and buttons, a buttoned tab, or a lace inset (Fig. 4-9).
✂ N O T E : When inserting lace, braid, or other fabric that adds width to the sleeve, measure half the inset width less seam allowances, and trim that amount away from each center seam edge.

■ FRENCH SEAMS OUT

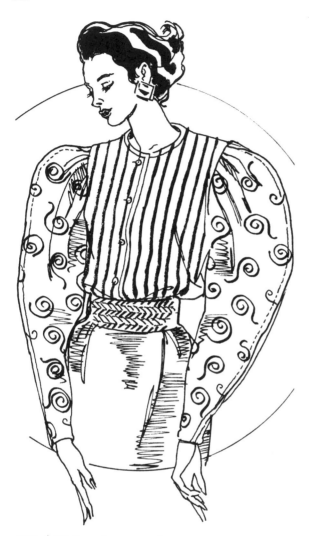

FIG. 4-10. French seams out.

There's more to a French seam than a tidy seam finish. Ready-to-wear designer garments are showing the French seam reversed, featuring the "wrong" side of the seam on the outside of the garment. San Francisco designers Jean and Marc created one of our favorite uses of this seam. The unique outward curve of the sleeve accentuates the reversed French seam (Fig. 4-10).

■ PATTERN AND DESIGN CONSIDERATIONS

1. Use a basic sleeve pattern with a fitted cap and adjust the sleeve length as needed for your arm length.

2. Mark the sleeve center, drawing a vertical line from the center-cap marking down the sleeve parallel to the grainline. Copy the grainline to both sides of the sleeve close to the underarm seam (otherwise the grainline will shift when you slash and spread the pattern). Cut out the pattern, slashing it apart at the center line.

3. On the back side of the sleeve pattern slash vertically. Begin at the cap halfway between the back notches and the center line. Slash straight down the sleeve to, but not through, the lower edge (Fig. 4-11). Position the pat-

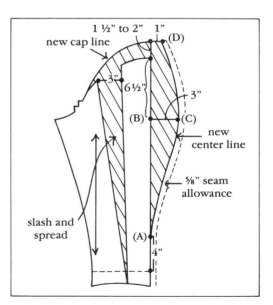

FIG. 4-11. Slash and spread pattern, then re-shape cap and center seam. Make adjustments for both back and front halves of sleeve.

tern over drafting paper and spread the slash 3″ at the cap.

4. Beginning at the hemline, measure 4″ up the center line (A). Beginning at the cap, measure 6½″ down the center line (B), then measure 3″ away from the center line (C), as shown in Figure 4-11.

5. Redraw the cap 1½″ to 2″ higher (or more if desired), then measure out 1″ from the top of the cap away from the center line (D).

6. Beginning at point A, redraw the center line through point C to point D, giving it a gentle outward curve. Add ⅝″ seam allowance to the new center line. Repeat the procedure for the front half of the sleeve.

■ CONSTRUCTION STEPS

1. Cut two of each pattern piece, using the grainline drawn close to the underarm seam.

Sew the center sleeve seam, using the following Design and Sew Tip for *Reverse French Seaming*.

✂ N O T E : The fullness in the sleeve cap needs an inner support to maintain its shape. You may choose to use an organza sleeve head or support the cap by backing the sleeve with fusible interfacing. If using the interfacing option, you'll need to apply the backing before seaming in Step 1. Refer to the Design and Sew Tip on page **60** to *Support Sleeve-Cap Fullness.*

2. Press the French seam toward the front at the top and bottom of the sleeve. Sew two rows of gathering stitches along the cap, beginning and ending about 3″ above the notches.

3. Stitch the underarm seam right sides together using a traditional seam. Topstitch or blind-stitch the sleeve hem in place.

4. Pull up the gathering threads and stitch the sleeve to the armscye, matching the markings. To add support to the fullness in the

---

DESIGN & SEW TIP

Reverse French Seaming

The French-seams-out technique is best suited for seams you want to draw attention to. Traditional seaming may be more appropriate for other seams, such as underarm or side seams. Be aware that the French seam does not work as well on extremely curved seams.

　　Place the front and back sleeve pieces right sides together, and stitch the center seam ¼″ wide. Trim the seam to ⅛″ and press the seam flat. Fold the pieces wrong sides together encasing the raw edges

of the seam (Fig. 4-12). Press so the seam line is at the very edge of the fold. Stitch the seam ⅜″ from the edge.

✂ N O T E : For a more dramatic effect, make a larger French seam. If you allow a 1″ seam allowance, you can stitch a ¾″ outside seam (instead of the ⅜″ seam described above).

FIG. 4-12. Place front and back right sides together and stitch ¼″ seam. Trim seam, fold sleeve wrong sides together, and stitch again with ⅜″ seam.

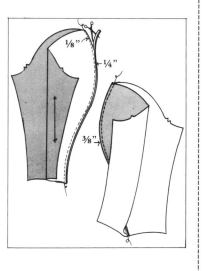

sleeve cap, follow the Design and Sew Tip below.

ENDLESS OPTIONS

The inside-out French seam provides unique emphasis to almost any seam. You can create the look of a piped seam in just minutes. Once again, the garment applications are endless. We like it on the waistline seam of a dress or the outside seam of pants. Remember to consider your figure type and whether or not the seam detailing is flattering; this technique will accentuate the seam.

Add your own fashion seamlines by cutting the pattern apart at the desired seamline. Add seam allowances to both cut edges and sew the French-seam-out to emphasize the custom detailing.

DESIGN & SEW TIP

Support Sleeve-Cap Fullness

Puffy Organza Sleeve Head— This technique is particularly suited for lightweight fabrics. To make a pattern for the sleeve head, fold down the top 5″ of the front and back sleeve patterns (Fig. 4-13). Position them together along the center line and trace the folded portions. True up the cap lines, then cut the fabric with the straight edge of the pattern on the fold. Leave the fabric folded and gather the curved edges together. Pull up the gathers so the sleeve head fits the sleeve cap area (approximately 4″ to 6″) and hand sew the sleeve head to the armscye seam with the folded edge toward the sleeve (Fig. 4-14).

Fusible-Backed Sleeve Cap— Back the upper portion of the sleeve with fusible interfacing. The backing provides ideal

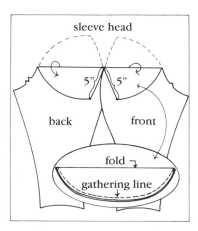

FIG. 4-13. Fold down top 5″ of sleeve patterns and trace folded sections for sleeve-head pattern. Cut sleeve head on fold and gather outside edge.

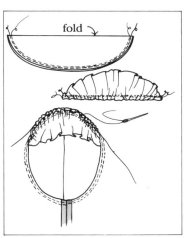

FIG. 4-14. Pull up gathers and hand-sew sleeve head to armscye seam with folded edge toward sleeve.

support for heavier fabrics. Fusible tricot works well for medium- to heavy-weight fabrics. Apply the interfacing before stitching the sleeve seams. Cover the wrong side of the sleeve cap to 2″ below the underarm or cover the entire sleeve. Before attaching fusible interfacing, pink the lower edge so a line won't show through to the right side.

■ WRAPPED AND BUTTONED FLANGE

This folded-over flange detail gives sleeves a stylish and flattering design line, as well as a custom fit at the wrist. This alteration involves adding a pleat down the outside of the sleeve and adding width to the lower portion where the flange wraps (Fig. 4-15).

■ PATTERN AND DESIGN CONSIDERATIONS

We prefer dropped shoulder styling for this sleeve variation, but any straight-sleeve pattern with a fitted (non-gathered) cap will do. The wrapped flange is ideal for a myriad of garment types, from basic blouses to oversized shirts and jackets or coats. This modification allows for numerous fabric types from lightweight sheers to heavyweight suitings.

Cut the sleeve pattern apart at the center and spread 1″ for the tuck. Tape the pattern over drafting paper and redraw the side seams parallel to the grainline (Fig. 4-16). This adds width

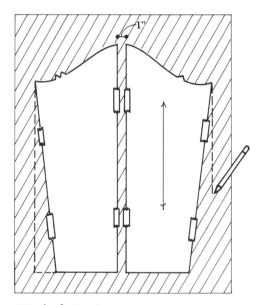

FIG. 4-15. Wrapped and buttoned flange.

FIG. 4-16. Cut sleeve pattern apart at center and spread 1″ for tuck. Redraw sides parallel to the grainline.

to the lower portion of the sleeve, allowing for the wrapped flange.

■ CONSTRUCTION STEPS

1. Cut out the pattern; then cut two sleeves using the newly modified pattern.
2. Stitch the underarm seam and finish the edges as you normally would. Fold, press, and topstitch the hem in place.
3. Mark and stitch a ½″ tuck down the sleeve center, making sure it is parallel to the grainline. Stop sewing the tuck at the hemline topstitching (Fig. 4-17). Press the top portion of the tuck toward the back of the sleeve.

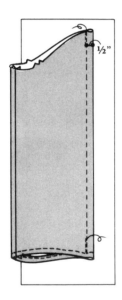

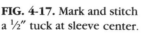

FIG. 4-17. Mark and stitch a ½″ tuck at sleeve center.

4. Construct the remainder of the garment and attach the sleeve following the pattern guidesheet.
5. Try on the garment and pin the sleeve opening partially closed so it is just large enough to fit your hand through. Sew the flange portion of the sleeve closed, stitching over the hem topstitching (Fig. 4-18).

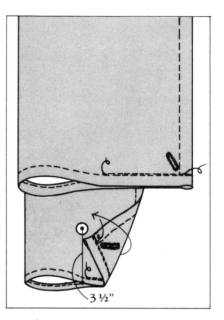

FIG. 4-18. Sew over hem stitching to close flange portion of sleeve. Fold flange toward front; mark button and buttonhole placement.

6. Mark the button and buttonhole placement. Position the buttonhole in the corner of the flange, angled as shown. Fold the flange to the front side of the sleeve and mark the button placement approximately 3½″ up from the hem edge.

ENDLESS OPTIONS

Embellish the flange with decorative stitching or trim, or just accentuate the line by stitching the pleat with decorative thread. Elegantly adorn the flange by repeating several decorative buttons up the stitching line.

■ BUTTON-ON, KIMONO-STYLE SLEEVE

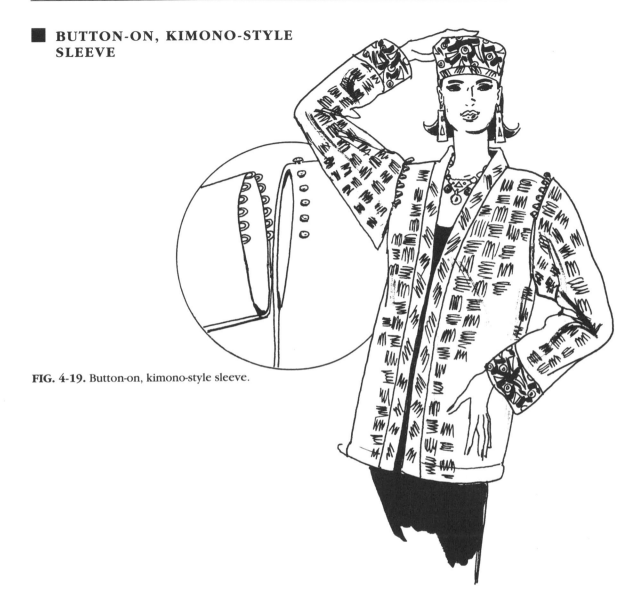

FIG. 4-19. Button-on, kimono-style sleeve.

You'll be the rage with this all-occasion, one-of-a-kind jacket. The kimono-style sleeves button at the shoulder. Colorful buttons and wild fabric are ideal ingredients for a playful beach cover. Or try jewel-like buttons combined with luxurious fabric for evening elegance. For easy yet high-quality construction, the jacket is lined and all the seams are hidden on the inside. The underarms are left open for comfort and ease of movement (Fig. 4-19).

This technique is ideal for medium to lightweight fabric. If using heavyweight fabric, be sure to use a lighter weight lining.

■ PATTERN AND DESIGN CONSIDERATIONS

1. Choose a basic kimono-style pattern similar to the one shown. If the pattern has a shoulder seam, eliminate it by overlapping the front and back pattern pieces at the shoulder seam (Fig. 4-20).

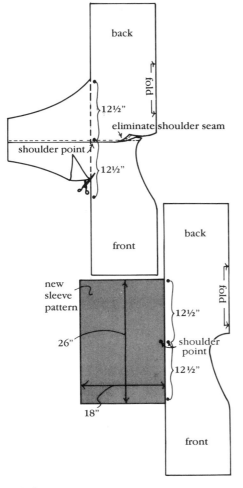

2. Spread the pattern out on a flat surface. Separate the sleeves from the bodice by drawing a straight line up the side of the pattern through the sleeve. Cut the sleeve apart from the bodice.

3. Draw a 26″ × 18″ rectangle for the sleeve pattern. The sleeve will actually be 18″ long and 26″ wide; the extra width makes a beautiful kimono sleeve. Adjust the length if desired.

4. Mark the shoulder point on the sleeve and bodice. Mark two points 12½″ from the shoulder point in both directions, as shown in Figure 4-20. This is where the armscye stitching begins and ends allowing for ½″ seam allowances.

■ CONSTRUCTION STEPS

1. Cut two sleeves and one bodice of lining, then two sleeves and one bodice of fashion fabric. Cut 1″-wide strips of fusible interfacing to stabilize the armscye and sleeve-cap edges. Fuse the interfacing to the wrong side of the bodice at the armscyes and the wrong side of the sleeve caps.

2. Position the lining and bodice right sides together. Stitch the front and neckline edges, the lower edges and the armscyes (Fig. 4-21).

FIG. 4-20. Eliminate shoulder seam on basic kimono pattern; then cut away sleeve from bodice. Make a separate rectangular sleeve pattern. Mark shoulder points on kimono and sleeve; then mark 12½″ to each side of shoulder point on kimono.

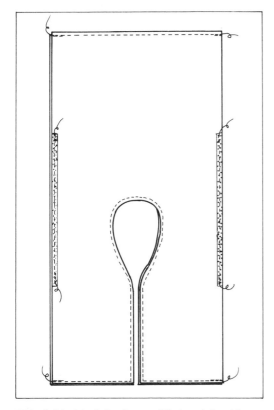

FIG. 4-21. Stitch bodice and lining right sides together, leaving side seams open for turning.

3. Turn the bodice right sides out by pulling the front sections through the inside of the shoulders and out through one of the side-seam openings in the back. Press the seams flat so the seamline rolls just slightly toward the lining side of the garment.

4. Stitch the front and back together at the side seams (Fig. 4-22). Begin stitching the lining front to the lining back right sides together, starting 2″ from the garment's lower edge. Stitch through the lower edge and continue sewing the front and back together. Stitch across the armscye seam into the lining, leaving a 4″ opening in the lining. Repeat for the other side.

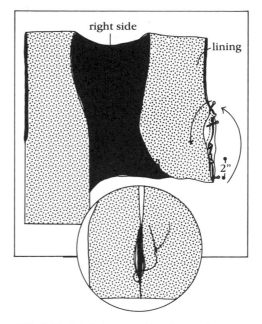

FIG. 4-22. Stitch front and back together at side seams, matching armscye seams. Hand-stitch opening closed.

5. Press the opening allowances to the inside, and blindstitch the opening closed.

6. To make the button loops, use rattail cording or construct your own self-fabric loops from fabric tubing. (See the Design and Sew Tip on page 45, *Easy Fabric Tubes.*) Cut 1″ to 1½″ tube lengths for each loop. The ideal length and spacing of the loops depends on the diameter of your buttons. Make a test sample first. Position the loops along the sleeve cap, beginning at the center marking and working out. Tape the loops in place just inside the seamline, stitch on the seamline to secure the loops; then remove the tape (Fig. 4-23).

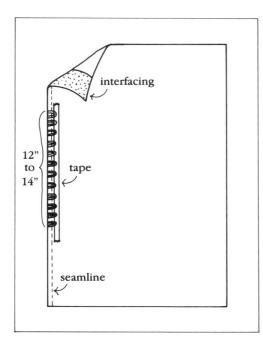

FIG. 4-23. Position button loops along the kimono sleeve cap. Tape in place to hold temporarily; then stitch on seamline.

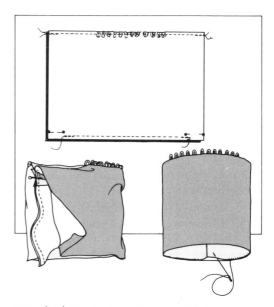

FIG. 4-24. Stitch sleeve lining to fabric at cap edge, catching loops in stitching. Stitch hem edge, leaving 3″ unseamed at each end. Turn sleeve right side out. Stitch underarm edges together; then handstitch opening.

7. Position the sleeve lining and fabric right sides together. Stitch the cap edges, catching the loops in the stitching. For added strength, use a short stitch length (18–20 stitches per inch) when sewing over the loops. Stitch the hem edges, leaving 3″ unseamed at each end of stitching (Fig. 4-24).

8. Turn the sleeve right side out. Fold the sleeve to bring the underarm edges together as shown in Figure 4-24. Stitch the underarm edges right sides together, beginning at the lower edge, sewing in a circle, and manipulating the fabric as you stitch.

9. Press the seams flat so the seamlines roll to the lining side. Press the allowances at the hem opening to the inside. Blindstitch the lower edge opening closed.

10. Sew buttons to the bodice armscye, lining them up with the loops on the sleeve cap. Wear the jacket with or without a sash.

ENDLESS OPTIONS

Opportunities abound by just varying the buttons, lining, and fabric. Consider inserting an interfaced tab in the sleeve cap (instead of button loops); then make buttonholes in the tab and you have a whole new look (Fig. 4-25).

FIG. 4-25. Button-on sleeve variation.

For variety, as well as added warmth, back the fabric with lightweight batting. Choose a batting weight that best supports your fabric weight. Test before purchasing by layering the lining, fashion fabric, and batting and by draping them over your arm.

■ PETAL SLEEVE

FIG. 4-26. Petal sleeve.

Gracefully shaped layers overlap like flower petals to form these elegant sleeves (Fig. 4-26). The pattern is adjusted to eliminate the underarm seam and create the petal overlap on the outside. Use a basic straight-sleeve pattern with a fitted cap.

ENDLESS OPTIONS

To create your own personal style, you can adjust the length, fullness, flare, or shape of the petals. For clarity, we've included instructions for these variations in the procedures below.

■ PATTERN AND DESIGN CONSIDERATIONS

1. Trace the stitching line of the pattern onto pattern drafting paper, ending the underarm seam 1½″ below the armscye. Transfer the pattern markings to the draft, including the grainline.

✂ N O T E : If desired, you may adjust the sleeve length by making the underarm seam up to 5″ long.

2. Mark the pattern ¼″ inside the *front* underarm seam on the lower edge. Redraw the side seam from the corner of the underarm to the marking (Fig. 4-27).

3. Mark the pattern 3½″ from the center-top point of the sleeve down the *back* side of the cap. Connect the *front* side seam mark with this mark, drawing a gentle outward curve. Cut out the pattern piece.

4. Create a separate pattern for the back side of the sleeve, following the steps above, only mark the *back* side seam in Step 2 and the *front* side of the cap in Step 3, as shown in Figure 4-27.

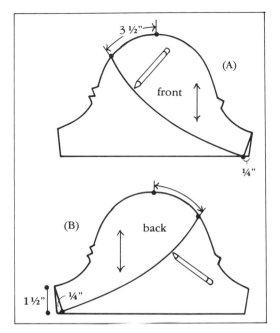

FIG. 4-27. Draw front and back petal sleeve patterns using original pattern as a guide.

5. For better fit, lower the front underarm curve by trimming ¼″ between the notch and the underarm seamline (Fig. 4-28).

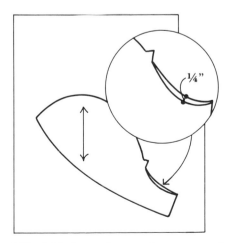

FIG. 4-28. Lower front underarm curve by trimming ¼″ between notch and underarm seamline.

6. If desired, make any of the following pattern adjustments:

Fullness—To add fullness to the sleeve cap, draw four vertical slash marks on the front and back sides above the notches (Fig. 4-29). Slash from the cap down to (but not through) the lower edge of the sleeve. Spread each slash ½″ to 1″ depending on the desired fullness. (See the Design and Sew Tip on page 54, *Slash and Spread for Fullness or Flare.*) Add 1″ to the height of the cap on both the front and back sides.

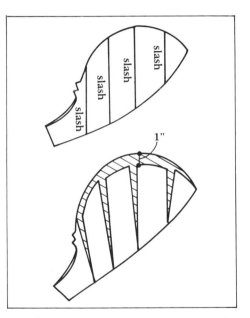

FIG. 4-29. To add sleeve-cap fullness, cut four slashes in both front and back, then spread slashes ½″ to 1″. Add cap height on both front and back.

Flare—Draw five, evenly spaced vertical slash marks. Slash from the hemline to (but not through) the cap. Spread each slash and add to the underarm seam so the sleeve makes a half circle (Fig. 4-30). Trim the front of the petal to create a gently rounded edge, as shown.

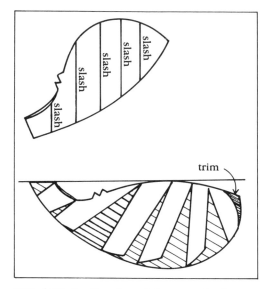

FIG. 4-30. For flared petal sleeve, make five evenly spaced slashes from hemline to cap. Spread at hemline so sleeve makes half circle.

Shape—Give the petals a unique shape by redrawing the outer curved edge of both the front and back pieces. (See the scallop-shaped edges in Figure 4-26.)

7. Join the front and back patterns into one by connecting the patterns at the underarm. When all the pattern adjustments are complete, true up the seamlines, add ⅝″ seam allowances; then cut out the pattern.

■ **CONSTRUCTION STEPS**

1. Cut two sleeves of fashion fabric and two of lining using the newly drafted pattern. Stitch the lining to the sleeve right sides together along the lower edge (Fig. 4-31). Clip and trim the allowances if necessary and turn the sleeve right side out.

✂ N O T E : If you prefer to eliminate the lining, hem the lower edge or serge-finish using a narrow rolled edge stitch.

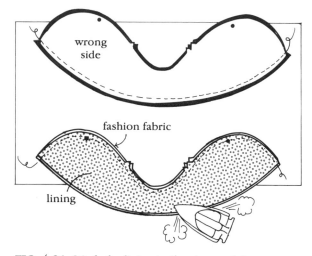

FIG. 4-31. Stitch the lining to the sleeve, right sides together along the lower edge. Turn to right side. Baste raw edges together at the cap.

2. Press so the seamline rolls to the lining side of the sleeve; then pin and baste the raw edges together at the cap.
3. Lap the sleeve back over the sleeve front, matching the cap markings (Fig. 4-32). Baste the overlap in place. If you added fullness to the cap, gather the cap at this time.
4. Sew the sleeve to the armscye following the pattern guidesheet.

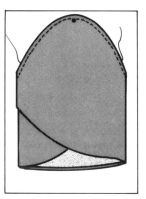

FIG. 4-32. Overlap sleeve back over sleeve front, matching cap markings. Baste the overlap in place. Gather cap if fullness has been added.

■ BELL CUFF

FIG. 4-33. Bell cuff.

The flared cuff with its wrapped-petal cut attaches to a fitted sleeve to achieve the most flattering silhouette (Fig. 4-33). Experiment by making the cuff and sleeve in same-color fabrics with varying textures, or try mixing prints and solids for a look on the wild side.

■ PATTERN AND DESIGN CONSIDERATIONS

1. Begin with a basic straight sleeve pattern; a gathered cap will work, as long as the lower portion of the sleeve is fitted and has no added detail.

2. Adjust the pattern length as you normally would; then cut off the hem allowance. (You'll add seam allowances later.) Mark the sleeve center, drawing a vertical line from the center-cap marking down the sleeve parallel to the grainline.

3. Measure 6″ up from the lower edge and draw a horizontal line perpendicular to the grainline. Cut the pattern apart at the line and use the lower portion for the cuff. Label the "front" and "back" sides of the cuff along the underarm seamlines, as shown (Fig. 4-34). Redraw the sides of the cuff parallel to the grainline.

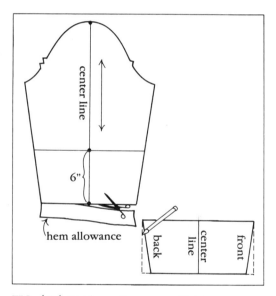

FIG. 4-34. Cut hem allowance off sleeve pattern; then cut off bottom 6″ for cuff pattern. Straighten sides of cuff pattern and label front and back.

4. Draw four vertical slash lines dividing the cuff into five sections with the center line in the center section (Fig. 4-35). Slash along the guidelines from the bottom of the cuff to, but not through, the top. Position the pattern over drafting paper and spread each slash 1¼″. (See the Design and Sew Tip on page 54 to *Slash and Spread for Fullness or Flare.*)

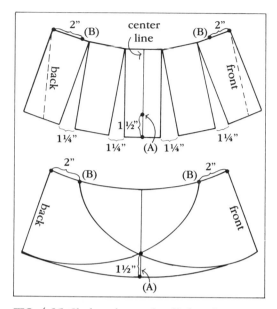

FIG. 4-35. Slash and spread cuff; then draw petal curves for front and back pattern pieces. Trace each separately to create front and back patterns.

5. Measure from the lower edge, 1½″ up the center line and mark the point (A). Measure and mark 2″ in from both sides along the upper edge (B). (See Figure 4-35).

6. To draw the petals, make two gently curved lines, one for the front petal and one for the back. The lines will crisscross, connecting the lower edge of the pattern with the center and upper-edge markings, as shown in Figure 4-35.

7. Trace the front and back petals separately so you have two pattern pieces. Add ⅝″ seam allowances to the upper and lower edges. Notch-mark the center line at the upper edge (Fig. 4-36).

8. Tape the front and back petal patterns together to make one piece, overlapping the underarm seamlines as shown in Figure 4-36. Mark a notch at the underarm seamline along the upper edge of the pattern. Draw the grainline parallel to the underarm seamline.

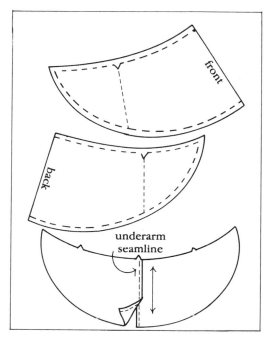

FIG. 4-36. Tape front and back petal sections together to make one piece overlapping at underarm seamline.

9. Add a ⅝″ seam allowance to the lower edge of the sleeve pattern. Notch-mark the center line at the lower edge.

■ CONSTRUCTION STEPS

1. Cut one sleeve and two cuffs for each sleeve.
2. Place the cuffs right sides together and seam the long curved edge. Trim and clip the allowances, turn the cuff right side out, and press.
3. Stitch the underarm seam of the sleeve and finish the allowances as usual.
4. Position and pin the upper edge of the cuff to the lower edge of the sleeve, right sides together. Align the underarm sleeve seam with the underarm notch on the cuff, and match the center mark on the cuff with the center mark on the sleeve (Fig. 4-37).

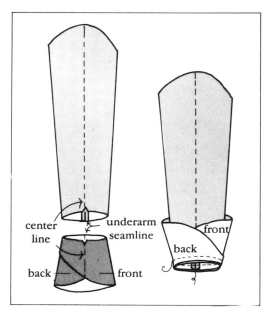

FIG. 4-37. Stitch the upper edge of the cuff to the lower edge of the sleeve, right sides together. Align underarm sleeve seam with underarm notch on cuff and match center mark on cuff with center mark on sleeve.

Overlap the pointed ends of the petals so that when the sleeve is turned right side out, the front side overlaps the back.
5. Stitch the cuff to the sleeve. Trim and finish the allowances and press them toward the sleeve. Construct the remainder of the garment and attach the sleeves following the pattern guidesheet.

ENDLESS OPTIONS (SEE FIGURE 4-34)
■ Accentuate the overlapping petals by inserting piping along the curved edge. Outline the overlap with buttons or consider a contrasting narrow ruffle or trim.
■ Emphasize the cuff seam with piping, trim, or a ribbon tie.
■ Our favorite is to make the petal from striped fabric. The grainline creates unique angles at the petal overlap.

■ PLEATED SLEEVE WITH FLARED HEM

FIG. 4-38. Pleated sleeve with flared hem.

Pleating adds a unique twist to any classic sleeve shape. The multiple-pleating is stitched with intermittent horizontal rows, creating a textured appearance. The pleats are left partially unstitched at the hem, giving a stylish flare at the lower edge (Fig. 4-38). (Technically, these are called tucks because they are stitched down the sleeve, but because they look so much like pleats, that's how we've referred to them.)

■ PATTERN AND DESIGN CONSIDERATIONS

Use a basic straight-sleeve pattern with a fitted cap and simple hem (no cuff) at the lower edge. Choose lightweight fabric and allow approximately 1½ extra yards for pleating. Adjust the sleeve length as you normally would; then add 3″ for the flare at the lower edge.

■ CONSTRUCTION STEPS

1. Cut a length of fabric long enough for one sleeve length plus 4″. The fabric will need to be approximately three times the width of the sleeve pattern. If your fabric isn't wide enough, continue the procedure and follow the instructions to add width in Step 4.

✄ N O T E : It's easier to hem the lower edge before stitching the pleats, but if you will be adding a width of fabric, you may want to stitch the hem after pleating.

2. Using a disappearing marker, mark pleat foldlines on the right side of the fabric with lengthwise lines spaced 3″ apart. Mark accurately for even pleating.

3. Press and stitch the pleats one at a time. Press along the marked foldline, then stitch *exactly* 1″ from the fold. Stop the stitching 3½″ from the end of the fabric and tie off the threads or backstitch to secure (Fig. 4-39). Press the pleats all in the same direction.

✄ N O T E : If you don't have a 1″ stitching line marked on your sewing machine, place masking tape on the bed of the machine approximately ¾″ from the needleline. Then measure and mark the tape exactly 1″ from where the needle enters the fabric.

4. If the pleated fabric is still too narrow for the sleeve pattern, seam an extra width of fabric. Position the seam on the underside of the pleat, as shown in Figure 4-39.

5. Measure and mark the pattern with horizontal stitching lines perpendicular to the grainline. Measure the first line 2½″ down from the cap seamline; then evenly space the remaining stitching lines (approximately 4″ apart) so the bottom line is 3″ from the lower edge of the pattern.

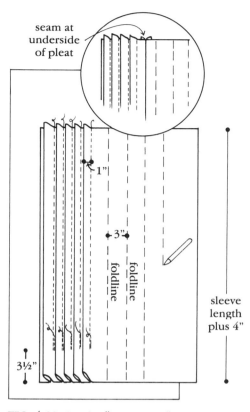

FIG. 4-39. Stitch 1″ pleats at 3″ intervals; stop stitching 3½″ from end of fabric.

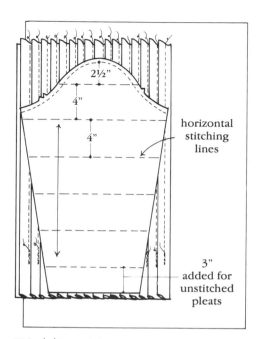

FIG. 4-40. Mark horizontal stitching lines on pattern. Position pattern on fabric and transfer stitching lines. Stitch along horizontal lines; then cut out sleeve.

6. Position the pattern on the pleated fabric with the pleats facing the sleeve front and the grainline parallel to the pleats. The lowest horizontal stitching line should line up with the ends of the pleat stitching (Fig. 4-40).

7. Transfer the stitching line markings from the pattern to the fabric using the same method you use to transfer dart markings. Stitch the horizontal rows, cut out the sleeve, then pin and stitch the underarm seams. If working with a difficult fabric, you may prefer to baste the pleats along the seamline first.

8. Repeat the above procedure for the other sleeve. Complete the garment and attach the sleeves following your pattern guidesheet.

ENDLESS OPTIONS
Consider making the pleats narrower or wider to fit your personal styling. Narrower pleats can be pressed in opposite directions between the horizontal rows of stitching. For added elegance, pleat the bodice front in addition to the sleeves. Additional creative touches may include edging the pleats with decorative stitching or trims.

■ LANTERN SLEEVES

FIG. 4-41. Fringed lantern sleeves.

The main part of these sleeves are graced with fullness, connecting to a slim-fitting cap to create a unique and flattering line (Fig. 4-41). Follow the general pattern adjustment steps below, then follow the directions for your favorite lantern sleeve variation—fringed, circular, or pleated. Be sure to allow for the added yardage requirements needed to construct these fuller sleeves.

■ GENERAL PATTERN ADJUSTMENTS

1. Use a basic straight-sleeve pattern with a fitted cap and no cuff (or eliminate the cuff and adjust the length). Adjust to the desired length as you normally would.
2. Redraw the sides of the sleeve parallel to the grainline (Fig. 4-42).

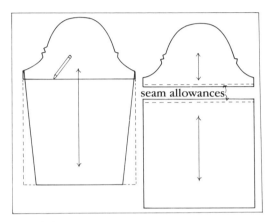

FIG. 4-42. Adjust basic sleeve pattern with vertical sides parallel to grainline. Cut apart sleeve cap and add seam allowances.

3. If joining the fullness into a cuff or band as with the fringed sleeve, adjust the lower edge for a custom-fit sleeve, using the following Design and Sew Tip.
4. To separate the cap from the body of the sleeve, draw a horizontal line below the armscye, making the line perpendicular to the grainline. The position of the line depends on the desired length of the fitted cap. Cut the cap apart and add seam allowances to both cut edges as shown in Figure 4-42.
5. Adjust the sleeve body, using one of the following techniques.

Custom Fit Sleeve

With just a simple lower-edge adjustment, the lower portion of the sleeve angles forward as the elbow bends for a graceful and conforming fit (Fig. 4-43). This alteration is attractive on many long sleeve garments and is particularly becoming to the fringed lantern sleeve. If using this alteration for the lantern sleeve techniques, make these sleeve adjustments before cutting off the sleeve cap.

(a) Draw a center-sleeve line beginning at the center cap marking and continuing down the sleeve parallel to the grainline.

(b) Trim off the hem allowance, then add 1″ to 4″ to the

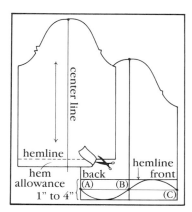

FIG. 4-43. Reshape bottom of sleeve so curve is lower in back and higher in front. Underarm seams should be equal lengths.

lower edge. (Add more length for lightweight fabrics, such as sheers, and less for heavyweight fabrics.)

(c) Draw a horizontal line halfway between the hemline and the lower edge. Mark intersecting points at the back edge (A), at the center line (B), and at the front edge (C), as shown in Figure 4-43.

(d) Draw a curve from point A to B to C. Curve the line down to the lower edge in the back and curve up to the hemline in the front. Make sure the sleeve's underarm seams are exactly the same length. Add a seam allowance to the newly drawn bottom edge.

■ Fringed Sleeve

1. Follow the steps for general pattern adjustments on page 76, modifying the hemline for a custom fit sleeve. Draw a cuff pattern, making the cuff circumference equal to the circumference of your arm, plus enough ease to fit over your hand and seam allowances. Make the cuff width 3″ or twice the desired width plus seam allowances.

2. Make spaghetti-tube fringe using the Design and Sew Tip on page 45, *Easy Fabric Tubes.* Use the sleeve body pattern as a guide and sew enough fringe to cover the pattern.

Overlap the fringe for a fuller look. For variety, make tubes out of contrasting fabrics and vary the finished widths from ¼″ to 1½″. Cut the tube strips on the straight or bias grainlines.

3. Cut one cap and one cuff for each sleeve. If desired, cut a sleeve body to line the fringed portion of the sleeve. If not using lining, trace the sleeve body onto water-soluble or tear-away stabilizer (plain paper will also work).

4. Place the lining or stabilizer on a flat surface with the right side up. Position the fringe

tubes over the sleeve body, pinning the tubes to the lining or stabilizer at both ends (Fig. 4-44). Be sure to position the fringe outside the underarm seam allowances. If overlapping the fringe, place fewer layers at the underarm portion of the sleeve. Baste the tube ends to the lining or stabilizer along the upper and lower seamlines. Trim the tubes close to the stitching.

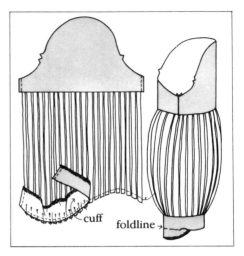

FIG. 4-45. Gather sleeve bottom and attach cuff.

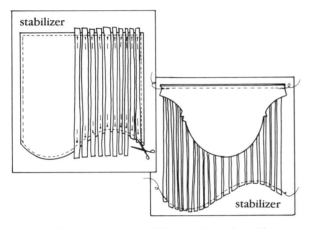

FIG. 4-44. Pin tubes to stabilizer (or lining) and baste. Trim ends, stitch tubes to sleeve cap, then remove stabilizer.

5. Pin the straight edge of the cap to the upper edge of the sleeve body with right sides together, sandwiching the fringe between the cap and stabilizer or lining layers. Stitch the seam; then remove the stabilizer.

6. Gather the lower edge of the sleeve body. Finish one long edge of the cuff. Pin the unfinished edge of the cuff to the lower edge of the sleeve, right sides together, adjusting the sleeve gathers to fit the cuff (Fig. 4-45). Stitch as pinned.

7. Stitch the underarm seam right sides together, being careful not to catch the fringe in the seam. If not using lining, stitch the seam at the cap and cuff. Fold the cuff to the wrong side and stitch-in-the-ditch to secure.

8. Sew the sleeve to the garment following your pattern guidesheet.

■ Circular Sensations (Figure 4-46)

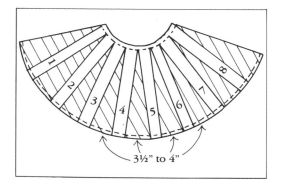

FIG. 4-47. Slash and spread lower sleeve pattern to create half circle. Add seam allowances to inside curve.

FIG. 4-46. Multi-layered circular sleeve.

1. Follow the steps for general pattern adjustments on page 76, drawing the lower edge of the cap at least 1½″ below the underarm edge. Eliminate the seam allowance at the top edge of the sleeve body.

2. Draw seven evenly spaced, vertical slash lines. Cut from the lower edge to, but not through, the top edge. Position the pattern over drafting paper and spread each slash 3½″ to 4″, then add to the outside edges, as shown, to create an approximate half circle (Fig. 4-47). Add a seam allowance to the inside curved edge and a hem allowance to the outside curved edge.

3. For each sleeve, cut one cap and one half circle. Staystitch the upper edge of the half circle along the seamline, and clip the seam allowance to the stitching. Seam the cap and half circle right sides together, pulling the curved edge straight to fit the cap (Fig. 4-48).

FIG. 4-48. Staystitch upper edge of half circle and clip to stitching. Seam sleeve cap and half circle right sides together, pulling curved edge to fit to straight edge of cap.

4. Stitch the underarm seam and hem the lower edge. Sew the sleeve to the garment following the pattern guidesheet.

■ A Flurry of Pleats (Figure 4-49)

1. Follow the steps for general pattern adjustments on page 76. Decide how far apart and how deep the pleats on the lower portion of the sleeve will be.

2. Mark the position of each pleat, then slash through the entire length and spread the pattern twice the desired pleat depth. (See Figure 4-49.)

FIG. 4-49. Pleated lantern sleeve.

3. Cut one sleeve body and one cap for each sleeve. Transfer the pleat markings, hem the lower edge, then fold and press each pleat into position. Baste along the upper edge.

4. Seam the cap and sleeve right sides together. Stitch the underarm seam. Sew the sleeve to the garment following the pattern guidesheet.

ENDLESS OPTIONS

Multiple Circles (See Figure 4-46)—Modify the circular lantern sleeve with multiple layers. Cut three or more circles for each sleeve. End the shortest (outside) layer just below the elbow and increase the length approximately 2″ with each layer so the longest layer stops at the wrist (Fig. 4-50). For more contrast, reduce the fullness slightly in the second layer and continue reducing it for each succeeding layer so the longest layer has the least amount of fullness. Attach them together at the sleeve cap.

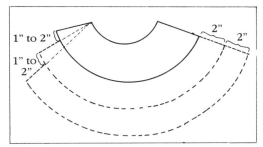

FIG. 4-50. Modify circular-sleeve pattern for multiple layers.

Stripes and Pleats (Fig. 4-51)—When making the pleated sleeve, use a striped fabric. Use the stripes as a pleating guide and pleat out one of the colors in the striped fabric. For example, if using a black-and-white striped fabric, make the pleats so the white fabric is hidden and only the black stripe shows. It looks like solid black fabric when the pleats are closed. When the pleats open up, the white stripes peek out from inside for a geometric finish.

FIG. 4-51. Pleating with stripes gives the illusion that a flash of color is bursting out as the pleats gracefully fall open.

CHAPTER 5

ORNAMENTAL OVERLAYS

Be your own designer with wonderful overlay additions. The possible variations are truly endless while the actual execution is simple. An overlay is basically an extra piece of fabric layered over the garment and sewn into one or more of the garment's seams (Fig. 5-1). By varying the texture or shape, the results can be dramatic.

Overlays originated with raincoats and parkas for the practical purpose of repelling the rain or snow. As fashion continues to evolve, this functional detail is becoming a hot new trend, moving from outerwear to day wear. What used to be a basic trench overlay is now appropriate over bodices, sleeves, skirts, or pants. Although the overlays can look completely different, the techniques are basically the same. Here are some general guidelines for designing and constructing overlays.

FIG. 5-1. Lace overlay.

■ CREATIVITY WITH OVERLAYS

There are many avenues for design inspiration. One of our favorite approaches is to design directly with the fabric. We like to wrap, drape, hang, or envelope the fabric around a dressform, a friend, or on ourselves in front of a mirror. The important thing is to have fun and let the creative inspirations flow. For additional ideas, flip through the pages of this chapter and review the colored illustrations.

Once you have a design idea, it's time to pull out the pencils and sketch pad. Draw the garment first; then draw the overlay on the garment. For easier sketching, copy one of the Designers' Templates in the Appendix, and draw the garment on the template. Then make copies of the garment sketch and draw numerous overlays, varying the length, width, shape, and fullness for ideal design proportions.

Choosing the fabric is one of the most crucial steps in the design process. You may vary the texture, such as with the lace overlay shown in Figure 5-1. Choosing a fabric of contrasting color, pattern, or weight can add unique variation. A very full sheer overlay is stunning when done in multiple layers finished to different lengths. You may choose to add texture and color by embellishing the overlay before you at-

tach it to the garment. For ideas, refer to
"Overlay Embellishments," beginning on page
119. Remember that overlay techniques will add
to the amount of fabric required for the garment
so plan your yardage calculations accordingly.

■ PATTERN CONSIDERATIONS

1. To make an overlay pattern, trace the original garment pattern onto pattern drafting paper, transferring the seamlines where the
overlay will be attached and copying the
grainline, notches, and other matchpoints.
For example, if making the overlay in Figure
5-1, trace the center-front, yoke, armscye,
and side seamlines (Fig. 5-2). If the garment
has a princess seam, the overlay may be
stitched into the front princess seam. The
lower edge of the overlay may vary; in this
case, we've positioned it 1″ above the waist.

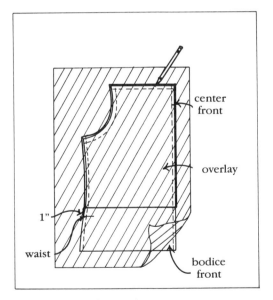

FIG. 5-2. To make overlay pattern, trace garment seamlines where overlay will be attached.

✂ **N O T E :** If making an overlay that covers two garment
pieces, such as one that wraps from the front to the back,
you may combine the garment pattern pieces to make the
overlay pattern, then cut the overlay in one piece (Fig.
5-3).

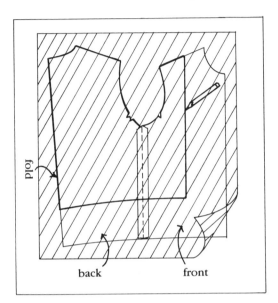

FIG. 5-3. For an overlay that covers two garment pieces, overlap garment pattern pieces
and draw overlay pattern as one piece.

2. Adjust the length and width of the overlay
based on the proportions in your sketch.
Draw the free-hanging edge as desired to finish the overlay pattern. (If shaping the free-
hanging edge, such as with a scalloped or
zig-zagged edge, draw the shaped details after adding the flare in the next step.)

3. At this point, you may add flare and/or fullness to the overlay pattern. Even close-fitting
overlays should have a small amount of flare.
Here are three options for adding flare and
fullness:

   Minimum flare—Flare for a fitted overlay
   can be added by simply extending the side
   seam ½″ to 1″ (Fig. 5-4). In order to hang

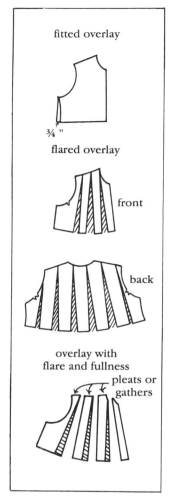

fitted overlay

¾ "

flared overlay

front

back

overlay with
flare and fullness

pleats or
gathers

FIG. 5-4. Extend side seam for *fitted* overlay. Slash from free-hanging edge to opposite edge and spread for *flare.* For *fullness,* cut pattern apart and spread for pleats or gathers.

properly, an overlay must have at least this amount of flare.

Added flare—To add more than the minimum required flare, slash the pattern from the free-hanging edge to, but not through, the edge that will be sewn to the garment. (See Figure 5-4.) The more slashes you

make and the more you spread each slash, the more flare your overlay will have. For example, a trench coat with medium fullness would have about 5″ flare, whereas a full overlay should have at least 8″ of flare. Add additional flare for lightweight sheer and lace fabrics for a dramatic look.

Fullness and flare—If desired, you may add pleats or gathers to an overlay to create fullness where the overlay will be sewn to the garment. To do this, first add the desired flare as explained above (at least 1″). Then slash from the lower edge through the pattern, cutting through the edge that will be sewn to the garment. Spread each slash evenly to give the desired fullness, as shown in Figure 5-4.

4. True up the seamlines, shape the free-hanging edges, and add seam allowances where needed, then cut out the pattern.

■ **CONSTRUCTION STEPS**

1. Cut the overlay from fabric. Finish the free-hanging edges using one of the following techniques:
   - ■ Topstitched, hand blindstitched, or serged narrow rolled hem.
   - ■ Bound edge with matching or contrasting bias binding.
   - ■ Enclosed edges constructed with a lined overlay or a narrow facing. This option is best for irregularly shaped edges.

2. Before constructing the garment, position the wrong side of the overlay to the right side of the garment and baste the layers together along those seamlines where the overlay will be attached to the garment. If embellishing the overlay, it may be easier to do so before attaching it to the garment.

■ OVERLAY-UNDERLAY VESTS

FIG. 5-5. Overlay-underlay vests.

Make two garments in one by attaching a vest into the shoulder and side seams of a blouse or jacket (Fig. 5-5). Sew the vest to the outside of the garment, creating an overlay vest. For those garments with center front openings, sew the vest to the inside to create an underlay vest.

These vest details are good-looking when sewn into T-shirts, turtle necks, silky blouses, or even jackets. Vary the length or shape of the vest to accentuate the layered look. The vest may be of woven or knit fabric and can be attached to a knit or woven garment. Experiment for an exciting look!

■ PATTERN AND DESIGN CONSIDERATIONS

1. Trace the front bodice pattern piece, transferring notches and other matchpoints. Draw the side and shoulder seams of the vest, using the bodice side and shoulder seams as a guide.

2. Draw the armscye, front, and lower lines of the vest, shaping the edges as desired (Fig. 5-6). In most cases, the vest side and shoulder seams should be the same length or shorter than the garment seams. If desired, use a favorite vest pattern as a guide when drafting the vest pattern.

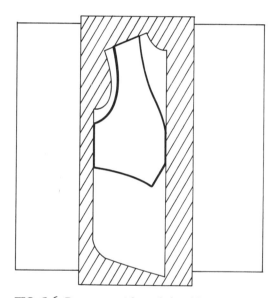

FIG. 5-6. Draw vest side and shoulder seams using bodice as a guide. Draw armscye, front, and lower lines of vest, shaping edges as desired.

✂ N O T E : Usually a vest lies over something longer, but you can reverse this. For more advanced sewers, consider making an underlay the same length as the original back-bodice side seam and shortening the garment front (Fig. 5-7).

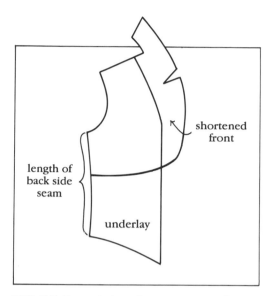

shortened front

length of back side seam

underlay

FIG. 5-7. For variation, shorten garment front and cut underlay equal in length to back bodice.

■ CONSTRUCTION STEPS

1. Cut two front vest pieces from fashion fabric. If lining the vest, cut two of lining fabric. Finish the front, bottom, and armscye edges of the vest with a fitted facing, lining, bias binding, or a rolled hem.

✂ N O T E : For decorative edging, make a reverse narrow-fitted facing from contrasting fabric; sew the right side of the facing to the wrong side of the vest; then turn the facing to the right side, roll the raw edge under, and topstitch.

2. Position the vest to the garment front. For an overlay vest, position the wrong side of the vest to the right side of the garment. For an underlay vest, position the right side of the vest to the wrong side of the garment. Baste the layers together at the shoulder and side seams.

3. Construct the garment following the pattern guidesheet, catching the vest in the stitching at the shoulder and side seams.

✄ N O T E : If lining a garment with an overlay vest, construct the vest as explained; then line the garment as you normally would. If lining a garment with an underlay vest, line the front before attaching the vest, then stitch the garment front/vest to the unlined garment back. Line the back separately, pressing the lining side seams to the wrong side and leaving the lining unstitched at the side seams. When finishing the garment, blindstitch the back side seams of the lining to the garment, enclosing the seam allowances.

V-FRONT OVERLAY

FIG. 5-8. Pleated V-front fan.

Playful pleating dotted with buttons gives a simple chemise designer flare (Fig. 5-8). This asymmetrical, V-front overlay has tucks radiating out to one side. Make this unique overlay from matching or coordinating medium-weight fabric that has body but isn't bulky.

■ PATTERN AND DESIGN CONSIDERATIONS

1. Choose a basic straight dress pattern with a back closure and standard jewel neckline. Because the design is asymmetrical, trace the full width of the bodice-front pattern onto pattern-making paper and transfer all markings.

2. Draw the overlay placement lines onto the bodice front pattern.

    Mark a point on the center front 1½″ below the natural waistline. Mark another point on the right shoulder seamline ¼″ inside the armscye seamline (Fig. 5-9).

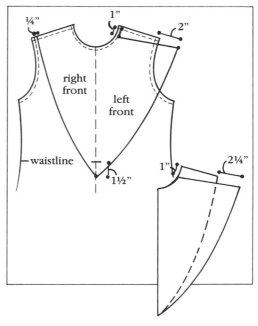

FIG. 5-9. Draw overlay placement lines on bodice-front pattern. Fold overlay pattern in half along center front to compare right and left sides.

Connect these two points drawing a slightly outward curved line.

✂ N O T E : We will refer to the right and left sides of the overlay and garment as if you were wearing the garment.

Extend the left shoulder seamline 2″ beyond the armscye seamline. Draw an outward curved line connecting the end of the shoulder seamline to the center-front mark.

Mark a point on the neck seamline 1″ from the left shoulder seamline. Draw a line connecting the end of the shoulder seamline to the neckline mark, as shown in Figure 5-9.

3. To make the overlay pattern, trace the overlay placement lines from the front bodice onto a clean sheet of pattern-making paper and cut out the overlay pattern. Fold the pattern in half along the center-front line to compare the right and left sides. Verify that the curves have a similar shape and check the measurement differences for accuracy, as shown in Figure 5-9. There should be a 2¼″ difference at the outside edge of the shoulder line and a 1″ difference at the neckline.

4. Draw six slash marks from the left side of the overlay to the right side (Fig. 5-10). Cut from the left side to, but not through, the right side. Spread each slash 1½″; then add seam allowances.

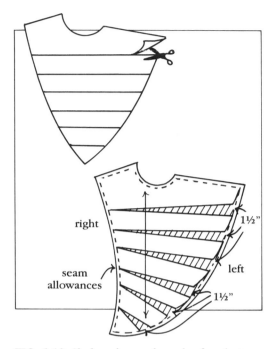

FIG. 5-10. Slash and spread overlay for pleats. Spread each slash 1½″; then add seam allowances.

■ **CONSTRUCTION STEPS**

1. Cut out the garment and transfer the overlay placement lines onto the bodice front. Cut two of the newly made overlay pattern.

2. Position and pin the overlay pieces right sides together, and stitch from the V-point up the left side across the shoulder to the neckline.

✂ N O T E : When stitching the corner, shorten the stitches for ½″ on both sides of the corner and make two stitches on the diagonal at the corner point.

3. Grade the seam allowances, trim the corner, turn the overlay right side out, and press.

4. Staystitch the right side of the overlay, stitching on the seamline with the wrong sides together. Position the staystitched side of the overlay to the bodice with right sides together, lining up the staystitching with the placement mark (Fig. 5-11). Clip the overlay

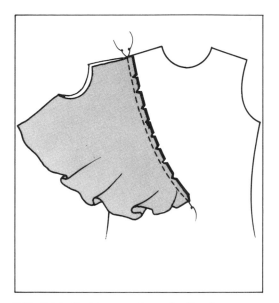

FIG. 5-11. Position overlay to bodice front, right sides together, aligning overlay staystitching with placement mark on bodice. Stitch.

seam allowance to the staystitching where needed to allow the stitching line to match the placement mark. Stitch.

5. Trim the seam allowance at the V-front corner so it will be enclosed when the overlay is folded over. Fold the overlay onto the bodice front so the wrong side of the overlay is to the right side of the garment. Baste the right shoulder and neckline edges together.

6. Working from the wrong side of the garment, hand stitch the bottom of the V for 1″ on the left side so the V lies flat.

7. Determine the button positioning and adjust the fullness of the overlay to form soft pleats between where the buttons will be positioned. Allow for more fullness at the bottom than at the top. We used six buttons and spaced them further apart at the top. However, you may choose to use more or fewer buttons and space them differently depending on how your fabric drapes. Experiment to see how the fullness and buttons will be

spaced. Sew the buttons to the overlay, tacking the overlay to the bodice at the same time.

8. Construct the remainder of the garment, following the pattern guidesheet and using the modified front. Be careful not to catch the left side of the overlay in the armscye or shoulder seams.

ENDLESS OPTIONS

■ A contrasting lining peeking out where the pleats ripple provides a pleasant surprise.

■ Purchase or make especially interesting buttons. Unusual shapes nestled between the pleats can be matched at the bottom of the sleeve.

■ Make the overlay from a companion fabric to the garment. A subtle change in texture made from a matching color is lovely. For example, try a silk-charmeuse overlay on a wool crepe dress or a crepe-de-chine overlay on a linen dress.

■ DOLMAN DESIGN

FIG. 5-12. Dolman design.

This asymmetrical overlay drapes over one shoulder and down the dolman sleeve (Fig. 5-12). Use any dolman-sleeve blouse or dress. You can easily spot a dolman pattern when the sleeve and bodice are made from one pattern piece and the shoulder seam continues down the outside of the sleeve. For the overlay, use medium to lightweight fabric with a fluid drape, such as a silky, soft rayon, or sheer wool. A varying texture or pattern in coordinating color to the garment makes an elegant scarf-like addition.

■ PATTERN AND DESIGN CONSIDERATIONS

1. Trace the neck seamline and center front line of the bodice-front pattern (Fig. 5-13). To draw the overlay pattern, extend the shoulder seam straight out from the neckline for the full length of the sleeve (the same length as the garment shoulder seam).

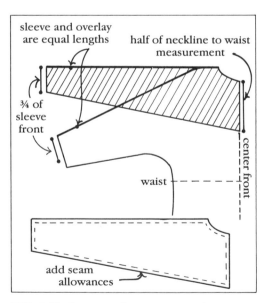

FIG. 5-13. Draw overlay pattern, tracing garment neckline and extending shoulder seam straight out from neckline. Draw lower edges of overlay and add seam allowances.

2. Measure the width of the front sleeve at the hem; draw the end of the overlay three-fourths this measurement. Measure the distance from the neckline to the waistline at the center front of the garment; make the length of the overlay at the center front half this measurement. Draw the lower edge of the overlay connecting these two lines, as shown in Figure 5-13.

3. Add seam allowances to all the edges and cut out the overlay pattern.

■ CONSTRUCTION STEPS

1. Cut the garment following the pattern. Cut one overlay using the newly drafted pattern.
2. Sew a narrow hem in the center-front and lower edges of the overlay (Fig. 5-14). Or, if desired, finish the edge with bias binding.

3. Position the wrong side of the overlay to the right side of the bodice front. Pin and baste the edges together at the neckline, shoulder, and sleeve hemline.
4. Construct the garment following the pattern guidesheet, catching the overlay in the stitching at the neckline, shoulder, and sleeve hem.

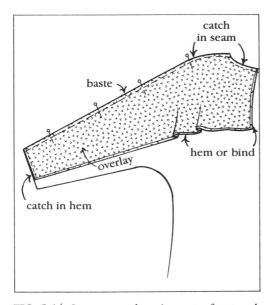

FIG. 5-14. Sew narrow hem in center-front and lower edges of overlay. Pin and baste remaining edges of overlay to garment at neckline, shoulder, and sleeve hem.

■ SLEEVE CAPES

FIG. 5-15. Sleeve capes: set-in, princess, and button-on.

Add a dramatic touch to a smart, business look. These easy-to-make, half circle overlays gently broaden the shoulder area for waist-thinning figure flattery. Sew the overlays into the armscye or princess seams, or button them on for show-off style (Fig. 5-15).

To create sleeve cape overlays, follow the general tips below and the specific steps for the cape you are making (set-in, princess, or button-on).

■ GENERAL PATTERN AND CONSTRUCTION GUIDELINES

Begin with a blouse, dress, or jacket pattern that has set-in sleeves or princess seams that intersect the shoulder seam. To make the overlay pattern, draw a half-circle that is approximately 20″ to 28″ along the straight edge and 10″ to 14″ at the widest point (Fig. 5-16). Adjust the size of the semi-circle, depending on the size

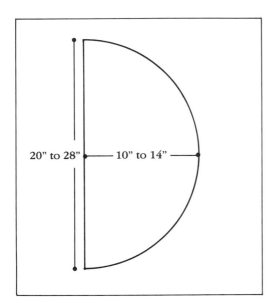

FIG. 5-16. Draw a half circle 20″ to 28″ at straight edge and 10″ to 14″ at widest point. Adjust cape size depending on size and style of garment.

and style of your pattern. To determine the best sizing, cut a sample in muslin using the largest measurements. Drape the muslin cape over a dress form or friend and trim the edges to achieve the desired look. Be sure to allow for hems and pleats or gathers where applicable.

Cut two overlays, one for each sleeve; then machine or hand stitch a narrow rolled hem in the curved edge of each overlay. (Or line the overlays; enclose the curved seam allowances between the layers and baste the straight edges together.) Cut the garment out following the pattern guidesheet.

■ Set-In Cape (See Figure 5-15)

1. Construct the bodice, except do not attach the sleeves yet.
2. Fold one overlay in half along the straight edge and mark the center point. Measure 1″

out from the center point and mark three 1″ pleats in each direction, as shown (Fig. 5-17). Transfer the pleat markings to the other overlay.

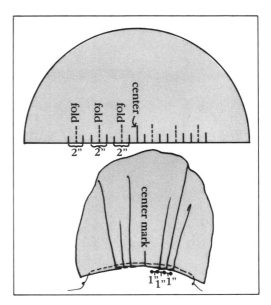

FIG. 5-17. Measure and mark pleats; then press and baste in place.

⚞ N O T E : Measure the size of the armscye above the notches. This should be about the same length as the cape's straight edge after the pleats are folded in. If not, make the pleats larger or smaller to adjust the cape to fit the size of the armscye.

3. Fold and press the pleats away from the center, pin them in place, and baste along the seamline.
4. Position and pin the cape to the bodice at the armscye, right sides together, aligning the cape's center mark with the shoulder seam. Baste.
5. Construct the sleeve and sew it to the garment following the pattern guidesheet, sandwiching the cape between the bodice and the sleeve. Be careful not to catch the loose portion of the cape in the stitching.

■ Princess Option (See Figure 5-15)

1. Stitch the center-front and center-back bodice pieces right sides together at the shoulder seams. Stitch the side front and back bodice pieces right sides together at the shoulder seams.
2. Position and pin the straight edge of one overlay to the princess edge of the center bodice, right sides together, centering it over the shoulder seam (Fig. 5-18). Baste; then repeat for the other overlay.

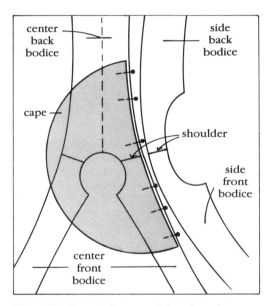

FIG. 5-18. Pin and baste straight edge of overlay to princess seam, centering it over shoulder seam.

3. Stitch the side bodice pieces to the center bodice piece at the princess seams, right sides together, aligning the shoulder seams and sandwiching the overlay between the bodice layers.
4. Complete the garment following the pattern guidesheet.

■ Button-On Variation (See Figure 5-15)

1. Construct the garment following the pattern guidesheet.
2. Fold the straight edge of each cape ¾" to the wrong side and press. Fold and press again; then topstitch to secure the double hem. This will usually provide enough stability for the buttons; however, if using very lightweight fabric, you may need to interface the hem before stitching for added body.

✂ N O T E : For a cleaner finish, hem the curved edge of the overlay after making the double hem. Grade the hem allowances at the corners to eliminate bulk. Press the hem in place, then squeeze each corner between your thumb and forefinger to determine the degree of bulk remaining. If you feel a ridge, underlayers may need additional grading.

3. Optional pleating: Mark the straight edge of the cape for pleats as done in Step 2 of the Set-In Cape. Fold and press the pleats away from the center, pin them in place, and stitch along the topstitching line to secure.
4. Calculate the buttonhole positioning, allowing for 5 to 10 evenly spaced buttons. The number of buttons used depends on the size of the buttons and your own design preference. Mark the straight edge of the cape for buttonholes. Mark the bodice at the armscye seam for buttons so the cape will be centered at the shoulder seam.
5. Sew the buttonholes and buttons as marked.

■ LUXURIOUS LAYERS

FIG. 5-19. Three-tiered blouse.

Soft, supple fabrics are especially feminine sewn in layers (Fig. 5-19). These tiered bodices are comfortable, easy-to-wear, and flattering for most figure types. Your fabric choice dictates dressy, casual, or even ethnic moods; wear these outfits to a wedding or a football game. With a loose fit, just a few seams, topstiched hems, and bound edges, you can make a layered outfit in one evening.

✂ N O T E : Consider your figure type to determine the most flattering layer lengths. For example, a layer ending at the bustline may not look best on all figure types.

■ GENERAL DESIGN CONSIDERATIONS

Experiment with the ideas in this section or create a novelty design of your own. Consider the following general design and construction tips for layers.

- Stagger the layers to different lengths for endless versatility.
- Add slits for an open, wispy feeling, while allowing for ease of movement and added comfort.
- We recommend lightweight fabrics, such as soft chiffon, batiste, cotton crinkle, rayon gauze, or challis. The sheerest of organza, organdy, georgette, tissue linen are more crisp, but are very appropriate for overlays and layers.
- For easiest construction, use a basic, loose-fitting T-shirt pattern and adjust for a pull-over scoop neckline. This eliminates zippers and buttons.
- The layers may be attached at the neckline with a bias binding, or the overlay can act as a facing, enclosing the neckline seam allowances when it is turned to the right side.

■ Three-Tiered Blouse

Multiple layers of sheer fabric over a favorite blouse are a stunning, yet modest, use for beautiful, see-through fabrics. (See Figure 5-19). Leave the sleeves single thickness for sheer, feminine elegance. Make the tiers of fabric on just the front or on both front and back.

■ PATTERN CONSIDERATIONS

1. To make the overlay patterns, trace the bodice pattern onto separate pattern-making paper. If making the tiers for the back as well as the front, complete these procedures for both the front and back bodice patterns.

2. To draw the hemline for the first tier, make a horizontal line perpendicular to the grainline about two-thirds of the way down the armscye (usually at the armscye notches) (Fig. 5-20). Draw the hemline for the third tier just above the waistline; then draw the second tier halfway between the first and third tiers.

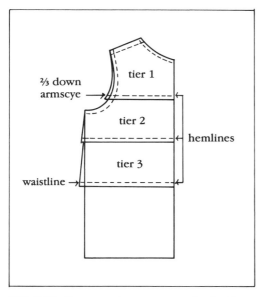

FIG. 5-20. Draw overlay patterns using bodice-front pattern as a guide. Add ¾″ flare at side seams and ½″ hem allowances to each tier. Trace each tier onto separate paper.

3. Add a ½″ hem allowance to each tier for a narrow rolled hem. Add the minimum flare for a fitted overlay to each tier by extending the side seam ¾″ at the lower edge. Trace each tier onto separate paper.

■ CONSTRUCTION STEPS

1. Cut one of each tier in addition to the original blouse pattern. Hand or machine stitch a narrow rolled hem in the lower edge of each tier.

2. Position and pin the wrong side of the longest tier onto the right side of the bodice. Repeat for the second, then first tiers so the shortest tier is on top. Baste the unfinished edges together; then construct the blouse following the pattern guidesheet.

■ Layers and Slits: Tunic Top
(Figure 5-21)

FIG. 5-21. Layers and slits: tunic top.

■ PATTERN CONSIDERATIONS

1. Begin with a basic, loose-fitting T-shirt pattern. Adjust the pattern length for a below-the-hip tunic style. Adjust for a scoop neckline large enough to fit over your head. (Refer to "Reshaping the Neckline," beginning on page 37.)

2. To make the overlay pattern, trace the front- and back-bodice patterns. Draw the hemline 10″ to 12″ shorter than the bodice hemline and add seam allowances to the center-front and center-back seams (Fig. 5-22). Add a small amount of flare by extending the side seams ¾″ at the lower edge.

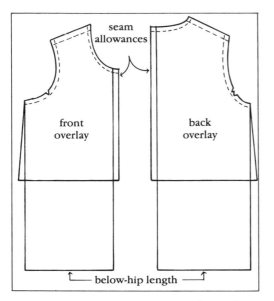

FIG. 5-22. Make overlay patterns 10″ to 12″ shorter than bodice patterns. Add seam allowances to center front and center back, then add ¾″ flare at side seams.

■ **CONSTRUCTION STEPS**

1. Cut two front and back overlay pieces. Cut one front and one back bodice with the center-front and center-back on the fold. Cut two sleeves.
2. Position the front overlay pieces right sides together at the center front. Stitch from the neckline down 4″, leaving the remainder unstitched. Repeat for the back overlay pieces.
3. Stitch the overlay front and back right sides together at the shoulders. Repeat for the garment front and back.
4. Stitch the garment at the side seams, beginning at the armscye and stitching to the waistline, leaving the remainder unstitched. Stitch the overlay at the side seams beginning at the armscye and stitching only 2″ down, letting the rest of the side seam fall into a slit.
5. To combine the layers, place the wrong side of the overlay to the right side of the gar-

ment. Baste the layers together at the armscye and neckline edges.

6. Construct the sleeves following the pattern directions. Set the sleeves into the armscyes of the layered bodice, treating the garment and overlay as one layer.
7. Bind the layers together at the neckline using matching or complementary bias binding. Machine or hand stitch a rolled hem in all the slits and lower edges of the garment and overlay. For neater corners, grade the hem allowances to eliminate bulk. Press the hem in place, then squeeze each corner between your thumb and forefinger to determine the degree of bulk remaining. If you feel a ridge, underlayers may need additional grading.

■ Asymmetrical Belted Overlay
(Figure 5-23)

FIG. 5-23. Asymmetrical belted overlay.

■ PATTERN CONSIDERATIONS

1. Begin with a basic loose-fitting T-shirt pattern. Adjust the pattern length for a below-the-hip tunic style. Adjust for a scoop neckline large enough to fit over your head.

(Refer to "Reshaping the Neckline," beginning on page 37.) Trim away the neckline or hem seam allowances if you will be binding the edges.

2. To make overlay pattern, trace the bodice patterns to make a full-width front and back pattern. Draw the overlay hemline about 10″ to 12″ shorter than the bodice hemline. Draw a vertical line for the left side of the overlay about 2″ from the neckline/shoulder seam intersection (Fig. 5-24). Add the minimum overlay flare by extending the side seams ¾″ at the lower edge.

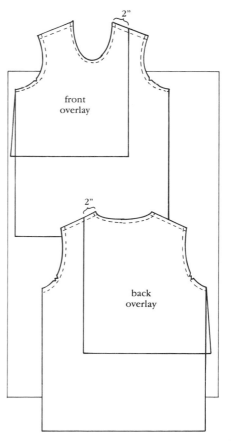

FIG. 5-24. Make overlay patterns 10″ to 12″ shorter than bodice patterns, with left side extending 2″ past neckline/shoulder intersection. Add ¾″ flare at side seams.

■ **CONSTRUCTION STEPS**

1. Cut one front and one back overlay. Cut one front and one back bodice with the center-front and center-back on the fold. Cut two sleeves.

2. Stitch the garment front and back right sides together at the shoulders. Stitch the garment side seams beginning at the armscye and stitching just past the waistline, leaving the remainder unstitched.

3. Stitch the overlay front and back right sides together at the shoulders. Stitch the overlay side seam beginning at the armscye and stitching only 2″ down, letting the rest of the side seam fall into a slit. Hem or bind the long left edge of the overlay; this is an edge that runs from the front over the shoulder to the back.

4. To combine the layers, place the wrong side of the overlay to the right side of the garment. Baste the layers together at the neckline and right armscye edges.

5. Construct the sleeves following the pattern directions. Set the sleeves into the armscyes of the layered bodice.

6. Bind the layers together at the neckline using matching or complementary bias binding. Machine or hand stitch a rolled hem in all the slits and bottom edges of the garment and overlay.

7. Make a 3″ to 4″ wide belt to connect the overlay pieces on the left side. To determine the belt length, try on the garment and measure the distance from the left-front and left-back overlays, allowing the edges to hang as in a tabard style. Attach the belt ends to the inside of the overlay.

■ Over-Bodice Sleeves (Figure 5-25)

FIG. 5-25. Over-bodice sleeves.

■ PATTERN CONSIDERATIONS

1. Begin with a sleeveless tank dress pattern. If needed, eliminate any closures and be sure the neckline is large enough to fit over your head. (Refer to "Reshaping the Neckline," beginning on page 37.) To eliminate closures, cut the pattern on the fold at the center-front or center-back, eliminating seam allowances or a button overlap.

✂ N O T E : If working with a firmly woven fabric that doesn't stretch to pull over your head, you may need to add a waistline zipper.

2. To make the overlay pattern, trace the front bodice pattern onto a large sheet of pattern paper. Trace the shape of the neck seamline of the back bodice onto the newly drawn pattern (Fig. 5-26).

3. The overlay pattern is shaped like a rectangle where the neckline circle is in the center and the shoulder line separates the front and back of the overlay, as shown in Figure 5-26. Draw the shoulder line perpendicular to the grainline where the shoulder and neck seam-lines intersect. Draw the lower edge of the overlay 1″ above the waistline. Draw the up-per edge of the rectangle the same distance away from the shoulder line as the lower edge is, making the back of the overlay the same width as the front. The length of the rectangle measures the distance between your elbows with your arms outstretched plus 2″. (This creates three-quarter length sleeves.) The ends of the overlay are parallel to the grainline.

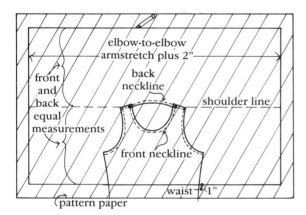

FIG. 5-26. Trace the front bodice pattern; then trace the shape of the back neckline. Draw the overlay rec-tangle so the front and back are equal widths from the shoulder line to just above the waistline.

■ CONSTRUCTION STEPS

1. Cut the tank dress from knit or woven fabric using the adjusted pattern. Staystitch the front and back necklines to keep them from stretching. Construct the garment following the pattern directions, leaving the neckline unfinished.

2. Cut the rectangle from overlay fabric. Then cut the neckline out, being careful to make the front and back exactly as marked on the pattern. Mark the positioning of the bodice side seamline at the lower edge of the over-lay rectangle. Sheer or very lightweight fabric works particularly well for this overlay op-tion.

3. Fold the rectangle in half right sides together and stitch as shown to create the underarm seam (Fig. 5-27). Stitch from the end of the rectangle to 2″ from the side-seam marking. Repeat for the other side of the overlay rec-tangle. If using sheer fabric, you may want to make these French seams for a neater finish.

4. Turn the overlay right side out and machine or hand stitch a rolled hem in the sleeve ends and lower opening. Stitch from each side of the lower opening up 2″ to form side-seam stitching, as shown in Figure 5-27.

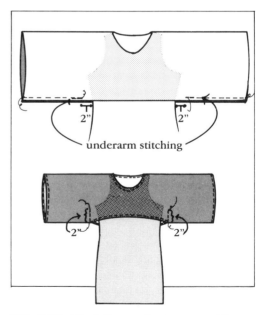

FIG. 5-27. Attach the overlay to garment for a self-faced neckline, sewing right side of overlay to wrong side of tank dress at the neckline. Turn overlay to right side and topstitch or un-derstitch.

5. There are two ways to attach the overlay and finish off the neckline edges.

■ *Overlay-Faced Neckline*—Position and pin the right side of the overlay to the wrong side of the tank dress at the neckline. Stitch, then grade and clip the seam allowances. Turn the garment and overlay right sides out and press, then understitch the seam allowances to the garment.

■ *Bound Neckline*—Trim away the neckline seam allowances of both the tank and overlay pieces. Place the wrong side of the overlay to the right side of the tank dress and baste the neckline edges together. Bind the layers together at the neckline using matching or complementary bias binding.

■ BODICE SCARVES

FIG. 5-28. Bodice scarf.

These elegant scarves gracefully frame the face for flattering, sophisticated style. The scarf overlays are sewn into the garment's shoulder, armscye, and/or side seams to create easy-to-wear, built-in accessories, ideal for those "I don't know what to wear" days (Fig. 5-28). The soft, fluid lines draw the eye upward to accentuate your face.

■ GENERAL DESIGN CONSIDERATIONS

We've included some bodice-scarf ideas you can experiment with, or you can create your own unique scarf design. Following are general tips to consider when making scarf overlays.

1. Use light to mediumweight, soft fabric with a fluid drape. Test the drapability by arranging the fabric over your shoulder or arm. Choose matching or companion scarf fabric or use the same fabric as your garment.

2. Draw the garment onto a copy of the Designers' Template in the Appendix. Then draw the scarf onto the garment, making numerous sketches to experiment and design a scarf with ideal proportions for the garment.

3. To incorporate fullness, such as pleats or gathers, slash and spread the overlay pattern. To add fullness to one edge (as in Figure 5-31), begin the slash from the edge to be pleated or gathered, cutting to, but not through, the opposite side of the pattern. To add fullness to the full length of the overlay (as in Figure 5-33), slash from the edge to be pleated or gathered to the opposite side, cutting the pattern apart. Make a number of slashes depending on the amount of fullness you are adding. Spread each slash, tape the pattern in place onto pattern paper, true up the edges, and add seam allowances if needed.

4. Large scarf areas provide a wide range of embellishment options. Possibilities include pinhead rhinestones, twin-needle or other decorative stitching with or without decorative thread, decorative fabric paint, or fancy trims. Let your imagination go wild. It is often easier to embellish the overlay before attaching it to the garment. (See "Overlay Embellishments" beginning on page 119.)

5. Finish the scarf edges with a machine- or hand-rolled hem, bias binding, or shaped facings; or, sew the scarf double layer.

■ Vested Scarf (See Figure 5-28)

This scarf is sewn into the shoulder and side seams of the garment. The armscye edge is hemmed and hangs free from the garment. The front edge is extended to create a tie. The lower and front edges are hemmed or bound.

To create this pattern, trace the shoulder and side seamlines of the front-bodice pattern (Fig. 5-29). Redraw the armscye so it is ½" to 1" larger than the garment armscye. Draw a horizontal line about 3" below the waistline to create the bottom of the overlay. Extend the lower edge 12" to 15" past the center front to create the tie. Draw the front edge beginning at the shoulder 1" to 2" from the garment neckline and curving down to the end of the tie. Add seam allowances where needed.

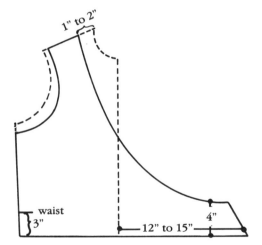

FIG. 5-29. Trace bodice shoulder and side seams. Draw armscye larger than garment armscye and extend lower edge 12" to 15" past center front for tie. Connect shoulder and tie end with gently curved line.

■ **Asymmetrical Drape** (Figure 5-30)

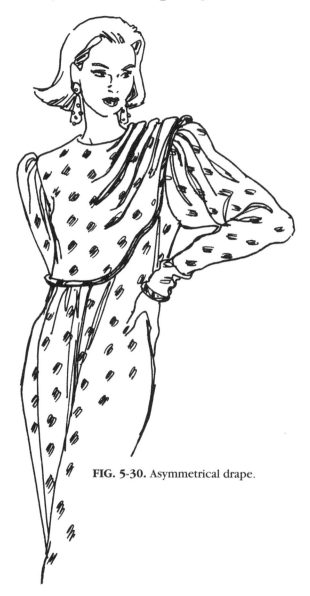

FIG. 5-30. Asymmetrical drape.

Show off a prize piece of fabric with this simple front scarf. The left shoulder is gathered, then the overlay is sewn into the garment neckline, shoulders, and right side seam.

To create the overlay pattern, draw the full width of the bodice-front pattern. Trace the neckline and both shoulder seams, as well as the right armscye and side seam. The right side seamline extends down to the waistline. Draw the lower edge of the scarf from the end of the right side seam gently curving up to the end of the left shoulder seam. Cut out the pattern.

Slash the pattern from the left shoulder to, but not through, the right side seam angling and bending the slashes to the side seam (Fig. 5-31). Repeat to create four slashes. Spread each slash 1″ (or more for added fullness), tape the pattern in place onto pattern paper, true up the edges, and add seam allowances where needed.

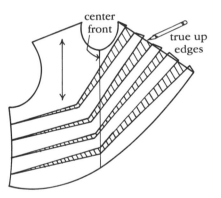

FIG. 5-31. For overlay pattern, trace bodice, drawing right side seam to waistline. Draw curve from left shoulder to right side seam. Slash and spread for left shoulder gathers.

■ Pleated and Looped Ties (Figure 5-32)

FIG. 5-32. Pleated and looped ties.

Wide strips of fabric are pleated at the shoulders, then sewn into the garment's side, armscye, and shoulder seams. The front and lower edges are hemmed or bound. The overlay is threaded through small loops that are tacked to the garment at the waistline.

Trace the side, armscye, and shoulder seams of the garment's front bodice. The side seam extends to 3″ below the waistline (Fig. 5-33). Draw a horizontal line to mark the position of the waist. The front edge of the overlay continues straight down from the end of the shoulder seam parallel to the center-front to about 12″ below the waistline. Draw the lower edge from the end of the side seam to the end of the front line. Cut out the pattern.

Slash the pattern apart, cutting from the shoulder straight down through the lower edge. Repeat to create three slashes. Spread each slash 1½″ and position the pieces on a clean sheet of pattern paper. Be sure to position the pieces so the waistline marking is aligned. Tape the pieces in place, true up the edges, and add seam allowances where needed.

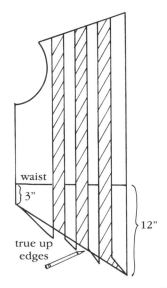

FIG. 5-33. For overlay pattern, trace bodice, angling lower edge down to point at center front. Slash and spread from shoulder to hem for pleats.

■ V-Front Tie (Figure 5-34)

FIG. 5-34. V-front tie.

This scarf is sewn to the garment's V-front neckline as a reverse facing, then is sewn into the shoulder, armscye, and side seams. The ties are cut long and embellished for added elegance. The lower edge and tie edges are hemmed or bound.

■ PATTERN CONSIDERATIONS

Use a garment pattern with a deep, V-front neckline. If needed, adjust the neckline shape. (Refer to "Reshaping the Neckline" beginning on page 37.) Trace the garment's neckline, shoulder, armscye, and side seams (Fig. 5-35). The side seam extends to 4″ above the waistline. Draw the upper edge of the tie beginning at the lowest point of the V-neckline and angling down just slightly as shown. The lower edge extends from the end of the side seam and runs parallel to the upper edge of the tie. Add seam allowances where needed.

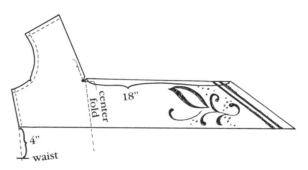

FIG. 5-35. For overlay pattern, trace bodice to 4″ above waistline. Add tie extension and seam allowances. Staystitch inside corner and clip corner to staystitching.

■ CONSTRUCTION STEPS

1. To construct this overlay, staystitch the inside corner where the tie meets the bottom of the neckline, stitching 1½″ in both directions, as shown in Figure 5-35. Clip the corner to the staystitching. Finish the lower and tie edges.
2. Position the right side of one overlay piece to the wrong side of the garment at the neckline. Stitch, then press. Repeat for the other overlay piece.
3. Turn the overlays to the right side of the garment and baste the edges together at the shoulder, armscye, and side seamline.
4. Construct the garment following the pattern guidesheet, catching the overlay in the garment seams.

■ Scarf Collar

FIG. 5-36. Scarf collar.

This sophisticated scarf has a cluster of pleats at the right shoulder and is pulled through a loop at the left shoulder (Fig. 5-36). All edges are hemmed except for where it is attached to the garment at the right shoulder.

■ PATTERN CONSIDERATIONS

To make the scarf pattern, cut a 45″ by 17″ rectangle from pattern drafting paper and mark lengthwise and crosswise grainlines. Mark off a 15″ area for pleating; then taper the long edges and end using the measurements shown (Fig. 5-37).

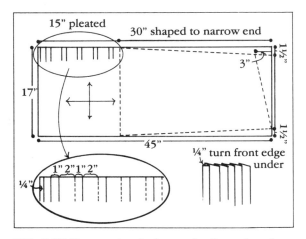

FIG. 5-37. Draw rectangle for scarf collar and mark 15″ area for pleating. Taper opposite ends to point. Hem all edges except 15″ area to be pleated.

■ CONSTRUCTION STEPS

1. Cut one scarf. Hem all the edges except for the 15″ area to be pleated. Hand- or machine-stitch a conventional narrow rolled hem or serge the edge using a narrow rolled stitch.

2. Use a blouse or dress pattern with a back closure and a faced neckline. Mark pleats in the scarf so the pleated area is approximately the same length as the shoulder seam (between the neckline and armscye seamlines). Most shoulder seams are approximately 5″ long, which would require 1″ pleats. Turn the front edge of the scarf under ¼″; then pin the pleats in the fabric. If needed, adjust the pleats to fit the shoulder seam. Baste the pleats.

3. Baste the wrong side of the pleated scarf to the right side of the bodice at the right shoulder (Fig. 5-38). Baste a loop to the right side

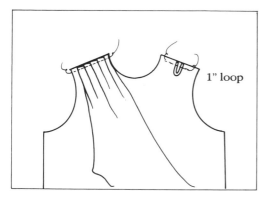

FIG. 5-38. Baste wrong side of scarf to right side of bodice at right shoulder.

of the bodice at the center of the left shoulder seam, making a finished 1″ loop.

4. Sew the front and back bodice right sides together at the shoulder seams, catching the scarf and loop in the shoulder seam. Attach the neckline facing and finish constructing the garment following the pattern guidesheet. Pull the scarf end through the loop and adjust the drape.

■ SARONG-STYLE SKIRT

FIG. 5-39. Sarong-style skirt.

You'll love the savvy style in this easy-overlay option (Fig. 5-39). Make this skirt in a single evening. Use medium to lightweight matching or coordinating fabric for the overlay.

■ PATTERN AND DESIGN CONSIDERATIONS

1. Begin with a fairly fitted, straight-skirt pattern with a back closure. We prefer this style without a separate waistband. Draw the full width of the front pattern piece. To draw the overlay pattern, trace the waistline and right side seam (Fig. 5-40). The side seam extends to approximately 10″ to 18″ below the hipline. The waistline extends 2″ to 3″ in from the opposite side seam.

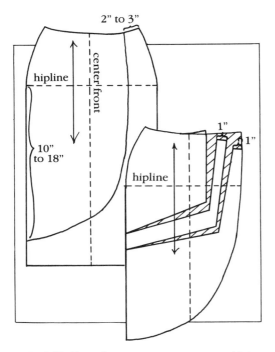

FIG. 5-40. To make sarong pattern, trace skirt at waistline and right side seam. Draw curved line from waistline mark to side seam mark. Slash and spread sarong pattern pieces for waistline pleats.

2. Make the lower edge of the overlay, drawing a gently curved line from the mark on the waistline down to the mark on the side seam. Cut out the pattern.

3. Make two slashes from the waistline to, but not through, the side seam, positioning the slashes about 1″ apart and 1″ from the outside curved line and bending them to the side seam, as shown in Figure 5-40. Position the pattern over a clean sheet of pattern paper and spread each slash 1″ to 1½″ (or more for additional fullness). True up the waistline and add a hem allowance to the lower curved edge.

■ CONSTRUCTION STEPS

1. Cut one sarong overlay, one skirt front, and one back, as well as the facing or lining pieces, depending on your pattern. Fold two ¾″ pleats in the top of the sarong, positioning them where the pattern was slashed and spread. Baste the pleats along the waist seamline. Hand- or machine-stitch a narrow rolled hem in the curved edge of the sarong piece.

2. Position the wrong side of the sarong to the right side of the skirt front. Baste the layers together at the waistline and side seam. Construct the garment following the pattern directions, treating the overlay and skirt front as one layer.

◼ TIERED HEMS

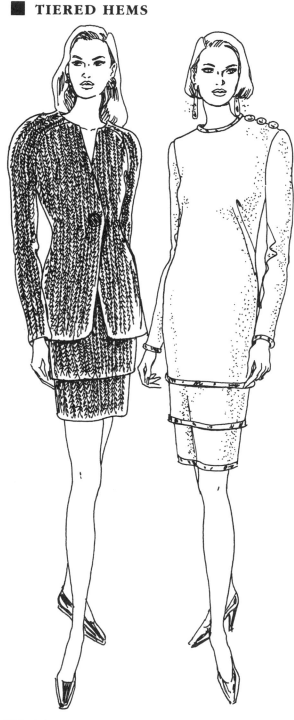

FIG. 5-41. Tiered hems.

These repetitive hemlines create a subtle rhythm that communicates confident style, a timeless option for a simple chemise dress or a basic straight skirt (Fig. 5-41). The underlayer is made from lining fabric with two fashion fabric layers stitched to the bottom of the lining. Because the underlayer is made with lining fabric, this option is ideal for lightweight as well as heavyweight fabrics. Three tiered hems are shown here, but even more layers are effective with some mid- to lightweight fabrics.

Use the lining as a single-layer base to which all the lower hemline portions are stitched. You can adjust each piece for the most pleasing proportions, experimenting with the amount of fabric that hangs below the upper tunic dress. For variation, consider making the tiers different lengths. We like the look of a middle tier that's longer than the bottom tier.

◼ PATTERN AND DESIGN CONSIDERATIONS

1. Before you begin, determine the number of tiered hems you'll have, the finished garment length, and the distance between the hemlines. These factors will affect how the pattern is adjusted.
2. Adjust the pattern for the desired finished length of the garment (the length of the longest hemline tier). If you will be binding the edge, eliminate the hem allowance.
3. Draw hemlines on the pattern to indicate the finished length of each tier (Fig. 5-42). Using a different color marker (indicated by a dashed line in Figure 5-42), draw another line 5″ above each hemline except the one at the lower edge. These markings will be used to create the outer tunic pattern, the lining pattern, and a pattern for each tiered hem. The dashed lines also indicate the stitching lines where the hemline tiers will be stitched to the lining layer. Repeat this step for both the front and back.

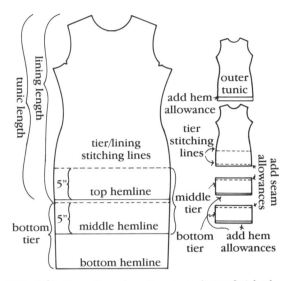

FIG. 5-42. Draw three hemlines to indicate finished layer lengths. Draw another line 5″ above top and middle hemlines to mark tiers. Cut separate pattern pieces for the outer tunic, lining, and tiers. Add seam allowances to lower lining edge and upper tier edges. Add hem allowances to lower edges of outer tunic and tiers.

✄ N O T E : The finished garment will have one outer tunic layer, one lining layer, and (in this example) two hemline tiers. Both hemline tiers will be stitched to the single layer of lining.

4. Trace the pattern to create separate pattern pieces, including one outer tunic, one lining layer, and two hemline tiers. Mark each piece to identify it. If creating multiple hemline tiers, you may want to number them. Add seam allowances to the bottom of the lining piece and the upper edge of each hemline tier. If you will be hemming the layers, be sure to add hem allowances to each hemline. If binding the hem edges, no hem allowances are needed. Complete this step for both the front and the back.

✄ N O T E : If you're unsure of how the layer lengths will look, make them longer than needed and adjust the hem-

lines later, after they are attached to the garment. This way you can try on the garment and experiment by pinning the layers at different lengths.

■ **CONSTRUCTION STEPS**

1. Cut out the garment, being careful to cut the entire outside layer in fashion fabric as well as the hem sections for the underlayer. Cut one of the front and back lining pieces for the underlayer, transferring the tier/lining stitching lines onto the right side of the lining fabric.

2. Sew the front and back of the tunic right sides together, stitching the shoulder and side seams (Fig. 5-43); repeat for the lining layer. Sew the front and back of each tiered hem section right sides together at the side seams.

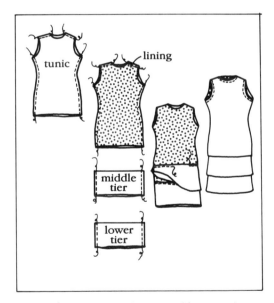

FIG. 5-43. Sew tunic, lining, and hem sections separately. Stitch each hem section to the lining and the lining to the tunic.

3. Press under the seam allowance of the upper edges of each hem section. These circular tiers are now ready to be positioned onto the lining base. Layer the sections, placing the wrong side of each hem section to the right side of the lining piece matching the tier/lining stitching lines. Topstitch the turned edges to the lining.

4. Layer the right side of the lining to the wrong side of the outer tunic. Baste the lining and tunic together at the neckline, armscye, and closure edges.

5. Construct the sleeves, neckline, and closure following the pattern guidesheet, treating both the outer tunic and lining layer as one. Try on the garment and have a friend mark the hemlines so each layer is an even distance from the floor and an even width all the way around. Hem or bind the edges.

■ THE LAYERED LOOK IN SKIRTS

FIG. 5-44. Sheer layers trimmed with lace.

FIG. 5-45. Fitted layers with slits.

Femininity is the focus of these long layered skirts. Consider sheer, lace-trimmed layers cascading with fullness (Fig. 5-44), or a fitted, opaque skirt with more distinction between layer lengths (Fig. 5-45). Modify the layer lengths, fullness, and slits for other novel looks.

■ PATTERN AND DESIGN CONSIDERATIONS

Use the Designers' Template in the Appendix to experiment and design the skirt you want. Choose a skirt pattern that is similar in style to the desired finished look.

Adjust the pattern length for the longest layer; then mark the length of the other layer(s) on the pattern. Trace the pattern to create separate pieces for each layer. Complete this step for both the front and back.

■ CONSTRUCTION STEPS

1. Cut out the skirt and sew the side seams of each layer separately. If the pattern calls for pockets, you may insert them in the outside layer. Finish the slits with a machine or hand-stitched narrow hem.

2. Position the layers together, placing the wrong side of the outside layer to the right side of the layer underneath it. Baste the layers together at the waistline.

✄ N O T E : If there is a zipper closure and the skirt is of lightweight fabric, insert the zipper treating both layers as one. For medium- to heavy-weight fabric, insert the zipper in the outside layer; then turn the edges under and tack the underneath layer(s) to the zipper as you would a lining.

3. Attach the waistband, treating the layers as one. Hem each layer separately, trimming the edges with lace if desired.

■ OPTIONAL CONSTRUCTION FOR ELASTIC WAISTBANDS

Complete Step 1 above. Fold the waistband over the elastic and baste the seam allowances together. Position the waistband to the right side of the outside skirt layer, aligning the waistline edges (Fig. 5-46). Baste, stretching the elastic to fit.

Position the wrong side of the under layer to the right side of the outside layer, aligning the waistline seam allowances and sandwiching the waistband between the layers. (If there are multiple *under* layers, position them together first, placing the wrong side of the outer layer to the right side of the underneath layer.) Baste, then stitch, the layers together at the waistline, stretching the waistband to fit as you stitch. Turn the layers right side out and hem each layer separately.

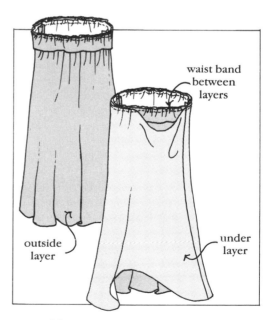

FIG. 5-46. Position wrong side of under layer to right side of outer layer, sandwiching elastic waistband between. Baste and stitch.

■ A SIDEWAYS OVERLAY FOR PANTS

FIG. 5-47. Sideways pants overlay.

Sew this sporty, geometric addition into the side seam of a favorite pants pattern (Fig. 5-47). For a more sophisticated statement, use wide-legged pants and soft, drapey fabric. Use matching or coordinating fabric for the overlay.

■ PATTERN AND DESIGN CONSIDERATIONS

1. Begin with any pants pattern. We like the casual yet classic fly-front closure, but a back closure will also do. Trace the front pattern piece onto pattern-making paper. To draw the overlay pattern, use the side seam and waistline seam as a guide. The overlay extends about 4″ along the waistline from the side seam; the side seam extends down as far as you would like (Fig. 5-48). Keep in mind that a longer overlay lends a more slimming, vertical look.

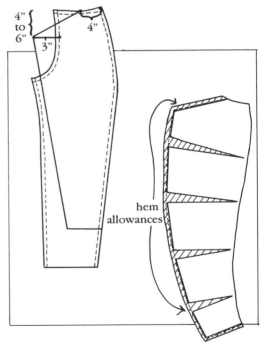

FIG. 5-48. Draw overlay following side seam and waistline of pant front. Overlay extends 4″ along waistline and down side seam. Make four slashes and spread each 1″.

✂ N O T E : These measurements are approximate. You may need to vary them depending on the length of your torso, inseam, and side seam; and on the style of the pattern.

2. Draw the front edge of the overlay using the measurements shown in Figure 5-48. The width of the lower edge depends on the width of the pant leg. You may want to hold the pattern up to you to make sure the angles create pleasing lines for your figure. Adjust the overlay as desired; then cut out the pattern.

3. Make four slashes from the inseam side of the overlay to, but not through, the outside seam, spacing them evenly apart. Position the pattern over a clean sheet of pattern-making paper and spread each slash 1″ (or more for additional fullness). True up the line and add a hem allowance to all the overlay edges except the outside and waist seams.

■ **CONSTRUCTION STEPS**

1. Cut one of the overlay pattern and cut out the pants following the pattern guidesheet. Hand or machine stitch a narrow rolled hem in the outside edges of the overlay (all but the waist and outside seam).

2. Position the wrong side of the overlay to the right side of the left pant front. Baste the layers together at the waistline and side seam. Construct the garment following the pattern directions, treating the overlay and pant front as one layer when sewing the waist and outside seams of the garment. Be sure not to catch the rest of the overlay in the stitching when sewing the other seams.

3. Try on the pants and mark button and buttonhole positioning guidelines. Sew buttonholes in the overlay as marked; then verify that the button marking is as desired and sew the button to the garment.

■ **OVERLAY EMBELLISHMENTS**

FIG. 5-49. Drawstring embellished overlay.

Overlays provide an ideal opportunity to show off your latest embellishment techniques: a set of beautiful buttons or rhinestones, some fancy trim, and much, much more (Fig. 5-49). Use any of the techniques in this chapter to create the overlay pattern. The ideal time to add most embellishments is after cutting out the overlay and before sewing it to the garment. If hemming or binding any overlay edges, do so before embellishing.

Some of the following suggestions may require pattern or construction variations, such as the drawstring overlay or the detachable overlay that buttons to the garment (Fig. 5-50). In these cases, plan out your pattern and construction strategy before making the pattern and cutting out your fabric.

Following are some ideas. The possibilities are limitless so we encourage you to be creative and enjoy (Fig. 5-51).

Lace, rickrack, or trim, sewn or glued to the edges.

Appliqués, grommets, studs, rhinestones, or buttons randomly applied.

Multiple rows of topstitching on portions of the overlay.

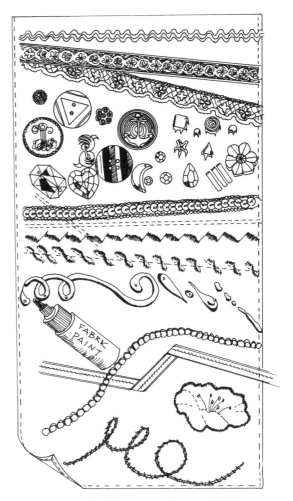

FIG. 5-51. Embellishment options are limitless.

FIG. 5-50. Button-on embellished overlay.

Twin-needle or other decorative stitching with decorative thread.

Fabric painted with a unique design.

Overlays cut from stripes or plaids with varied grainlines for playful design.

Multiple pleats or an inverted center pleat.

Multiple overlay layers finished to different lengths.

Notched cutouts in the fabric edge dotted with decorative buttons.

Border-print fabric with the decorative border at the overlay edge.

Tabs and buttons or loops and lacing to draw in added fullness.

Shaped edges such as points or scallops. (Shapes usually require a fitted facing or lining.)

Drawstrings threaded through the overlay hem. (See Figure 5-49.)

Detachable overlays that button or zip to the garment. (See Figure 5-50.)

Decoratively shaped cutouts randomly positioned.

Lace inserts placed in a cutout or as a gathered strip (also called ruching).

CHAPTER 6

CUSTOM CLOSURES

Closures create a focal point in garment design. In most cases, they are literally at the center of the garment, giving you the unique option of making an entire design statement by simply varying the closure. In many cases, you'll want to design the entire garment around the closure. For example, the open-seam buttonhole detail allows you to position interesting design lines (decorative seamlines) in the buttonhole area of the garment; buttonholes are then made from small button-sized openings (unstitched portions) in the seamlines.

For refreshing repetition, closure details can be duplicated elsewhere on the garment, such as on the sleeves or pocket. Belts, tabs, ties, buttons, drawstrings, chains, and shaped edges are just the beginning of closure design. The variations we've shown in this chapter are only a fragment of the possibilities for creativity with closures.

■ OPEN-SEAM BUTTONHOLES

FIG. 6-1. Open-seam buttonholes.

The buttons on this garment appear to dance with the design (Fig. 6-1). Seams are added to create new design lines in the garment as well as buttonholes made from gaps or unstitched portions of the seam. You can add straight or curved design lines anywhere on the garment by simply cutting the pattern apart and adding seam allowances.

■ DESIGN AND PATTERN CONSIDERATIONS

1. Use the Designers' Template in the Appendix to determine the placement of design-line seams. Draw the design lines on the garment, experimenting for the most desirable arrangement. Because the buttonholes will be in the seams, the design lines must intersect with the desired buttonhole positions.

2. When you've decided on the finished design, draw the seamlines onto the garment pattern using the template sketch as a guide. To keep the original pattern intact, you may want to trace the pattern first, then work with the traced copy of the pattern.

3. Mark the buttonhole positions on the newly marked seamlines. Cut the pattern apart on the design lines and add seam allowances to both cut edges. If the pattern is being divided into many pieces, number them to keep them organized (Fig. 6-2).

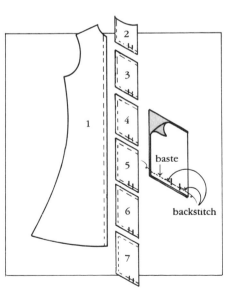

FIG. 6-2. Number pattern pieces and mark buttonhole positions; then cut pattern apart and add seam allowances. When stitching, backstitch before and after buttonholes and baste across buttonholes.

■ **CONSTRUCTION STEPS**

1. Cut out the garment using the newly adjusted pattern pieces. For variety, use contrasting fabrics or cut the pieces on different grainlines for a chevron effect. Be sure to transfer the buttonhole markings accurately.

2. Stitch the garment pieces right sides together at the design-line seams. When you get to a buttonhole marking, backstitch just before the buttonhole; then baste across the buttonhole and backstitch again just after the buttonhole, as shown in Figure 6-2. Continue stitching the seam, backstitching before and after each buttonhole opening if there are additional buttonholes in that seam.

3. Press the seams flat on both sides to set the stitching; then press the seam allowances open.

4. Mark the buttonhole positions on the facing pieces. Then, make faced slits (see Design and Sew Tip, *Facing a Slit Opening*) to correspond to the buttonhole openings (Fig. 6-3).

5. Construct the rest of the garment following the pattern guidesheet and using the adjusted bodice and facing pieces.

6. Remove the basting stitches in the buttonhole portions of the seams. Hand tack the facing to the garment at the buttonholes, aligning the faced slits with the open-seam buttonholes. Try on the garment to mark the button positions, then sew the buttons on as marked.

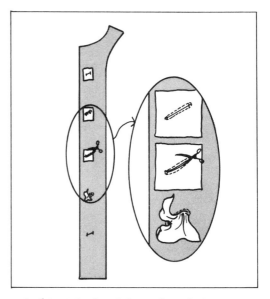

FIG. 6-3. Make faced slits in front facing to correspond to buttonhole openings.

DESIGN & SEW TIP

Facing a Slit Opening

Cut a stay from lightweight fabric such as organza, about 1″ to 2″ longer and wider than the slit area. Position the stay to the right side of the facing fabric over the slit marking. If you can't see through the stay material, transfer the slit markings.

✂ N O T E : Consider using fusible interfacing for the stay instead of organza. Position the non-fusible side to the right side of the fabric; then fuse the stay in place after turning it to the wrong side.

Using a short stitch length (12 to 20 stitches per inch), sew around slit markings, stitching just outside the line and curving around ends. Cut through center of slits, clipping carefully into each corner. Turn the stay through opening to wrong side and press, rolling seam toward the wrong side.

WINDOW-WELT BUTTONHOLES

FIG. 6-4. Window-welt buttonholes.

Customize your favorite pattern with these window-welt buttonholes (Fig. 6-4). The welts showing through the window create in-seam buttonholes. For added novelty, vary the shape and size of the window, the position of the window on the garment, and the fabric used to create the welts.

■ PATTERN AND DESIGN CONSIDERATIONS

Use the Designers' Template in the Appendix to design the shape and placement of the windows. Sketch the desired shape, position, and proportionate size of the window. Draw the welt line and button placement in the window as well. Usually the welts are centered in the window, but this is not necessary.

When you've decided on the finished design, draw window and buttonhole placement lines onto the garment pattern using the template sketch as a guide.

■ CONSTRUCTION STEPS

1. Cut out your garment following the pattern guidesheet. Transfer the window and welt placement lines onto the right side of the garment.
2. Stabilize the garment by backing the window area with fusible interfacing. The interfacing should be about 1″ larger than the window on all sides.
3. Make a window stay from lightweight fabric such as organza. Cut the stay about 2″ longer and wider than the window and mark the exact window shape onto the stay. Position and pin the stay to the right side of the garment, aligning the window markings.
4. Stitch along the stay markings using a short stitch length (12 to 20 stitches per inch) and taking one stitch across each corner.
5. Cut through the center of the window, clipping carefully into each corner (Fig. 6-5). Turn the stay through the window to the wrong side and press, rolling the seam to the wrong side as you press.

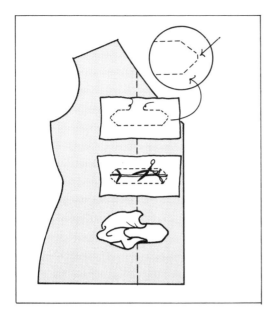

FIG. 6-5. Make window opening by stitching window shape through organza and garment fabric. Cut center of window to corners and turn stay to wrong side.

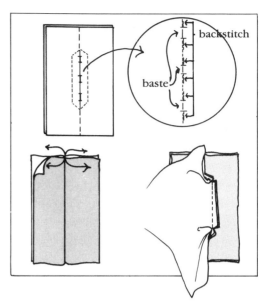

FIG. 6-6. Mark center of welt rectangles and buttonhole placement. Stitch center line, basting across buttonholes. Press rectangles away from each other. Center welts behind window, fold garment back, and stitch over original stitching.

6. To make the welts, cut two rectangles 3″ longer and 3″ wider than the window. Use contrasting fabric if desired; Ultraleather is one of our favorite options. If using lightweight fabric for the welts, fuse interfacing to the wrong side for added stability.

7. Mark the center line of each welt rectangle and mark the exact buttonhole placement on that center line (Fig. 6-6). Pin the welts right sides together and begin stitching along the center line. When you get to the first buttonhole marking, backstitch just before the mark, then baste across the buttonhole and backstitch again just after the buttonhole marking. Continue stitching the rectangles together, backstitching before and after each buttonhole marking.

8. Press the rectangles flat to set the stitching; then press them away from each other, as shown in Figure 6-6, to form the welts.

9. Center the welts over the wrong side of the window and tape them in place from the right side. (We recommend Scotch Magic tape or drafting tape.) Fold the garment back to expose the first set of stitching used to secure the stay. Stitch again over the first set of stitches, sewing through the welts. Continue folding back the garment and stitching until all sides of the window have been stitched through the welts.

10. To finish the wrong side, make a window in the lining or facing. Transfer the window markings to the facing or lining piece, then following Steps 3 through 5 above to construct the window.

11. Repeat the procedure for any additional windows. Hand tack the windows in the lining or facing to the wrong side of the welts. Remove the basting stitches in the buttonhole portions of the welt seam. Try on the garment to mark the button positions; then sew the buttons on as marked.

■ CROSS-FRONT CLOSURE

FIG. 6-7. Cross-front closure.

Graphically shaped front edges overlap through a slit to create this unique double-breasted closure (Fig. 6-7). Collarless, cardigan-style jacket patterns with few seams or design lines are ideal candidates for this closure.

■ PATTERN AND DESIGN CONSIDERATIONS

1. Use the Designers' Template in the Appendix to determine the shaping of the front edges. Draw the front edge with one or more pointed extensions, making a gradual curve to the shoulder seam and the hemline. Experiment by varying the curves, as well as the size and shape of the extension.
2. To keep the original pattern intact, trace the pattern; then work with the traced copy of the pattern. When you've decided on the finished look, reshape the front edge of the pattern using the template sketch as a guide.
3. Make two patterns for the right and left fronts, marking the center-front line on both patterns. On a flat surface, overlap the two fronts with the right front over the left so the

center lines match. Determine a pleasing position for the slit where the left front will
weave to the outside of the right front. Draw
the slit location on the right-front pattern. If
you have more than one extension, repeat
this for each extension.

■ CONSTRUCTION STEPS

We recommend making this closure using a
double-front (two layer) construction method.
This is a wonderful technique even if you aren't
making a cross-front extension. Use it whenever
reshaping the garment front or even for plain-
front garments. It eliminates the need for facings
and is especially good for see-through fabrics.
The second front is treated like a "self lining"
throughout the construction of the garment. If
your garment is made with heavyweight fabric,
you may choose to make the inside layer from a
lighter weight, compatible fabric.

1. Cut two of each front pattern piece (one for
   the inside layer and one for the outer layer).
   Transfer the slit markings to both right-front
   layers.
2. To make the faced slits, cut two 2"-wide
   strips of lightweight fusible interfacing the
   length of the slit plus 2", one for each right-
   front layer (Fig. 6-8). Follow the Design and
   Sew Tip on page 124 for *Facing a Slit
   Opening*. Remember to make slits ONLY in
   the right front pieces.

✄ **NOTE:** If desired, use lightweight fabric, such as organza, instead of fusible interfacing. Although using a
fusible keeps the slit facing from rolling to the right side,
it may make a ridge that shows through on some lighter-
weight fabrics.

3. Repeat the procedure to make a slit in the
   under layer, or if you have more than one slit
   in the garment, to make additional slits in
   both layers.

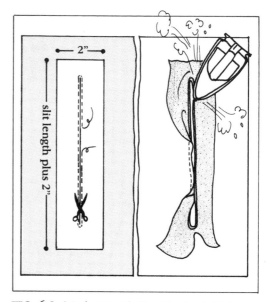

FIG. 6-8. Stitch around slit with short stitches.
Cut through center, turn to wrong side, and
fuse in place.

4. Sew the front pieces and their corresponding
   inside layers right sides together, stitching at
   the center-front and lower edges and stopping ⅝" from the ends (Fig. 6-9). When
   sewing the right front, be sure to align the
   slits. Grade and clip the seam allowances,
   turn right side out, and press. Hand tack the
   right-front layers together at the slit(s).
5. Hem the lower edge of the garment back so
   the length of the side seamline equals that of
   the front. Sew the front to the back, right
   sides together, at the shoulder and side
   seams, leaving the inside layer unstitched.
6. Press the shoulder and side seam allowances
   of the garment toward the front and press the
   shoulder and side seam allowances of the inside layer to the wrong side as shown in
   Figure 6-9. Position the inside layer over the
   garment seam allowances and slipstitch.
7. Sew buttonholes in the front extensions and
   sew buttons onto jacket.

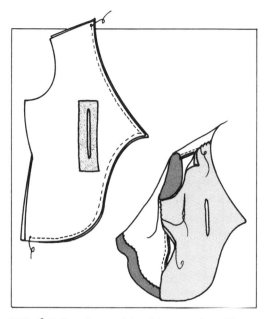

FIG. 6-9. Sew fronts right sides together. Turn right side out. Stitch shoulder and side seams, leaving inside layer unstitched. hand tack inside layer.

ENDLESS OPTIONS

There's so much you can do by making a few simple variations. We made this garment in Guatamalan Ikat fabric that had a subtle stripe. (See Figure 6-7.) Instead of making a faced slit, we added vertical seams, leaving part of the right-front seam unstitched to create the overlap opening (as explained for Open-Seam Buttonholes on page 123). Adding seams and changing the grainlines creates a unique chevron effect. Piping accentuates the vertical seams and specialty buttons provide the perfect finishing touch.

■ TABS, TIES, AND BELTS

Looking for a little fashion finesse? These closure details are for you (Fig. 6-10). Tabs, ties,
and belts are easy to construct and so versatile.
Make them any size or shape, construct them
from any fabric, and place them anywhere on
the garment. Buckle, button, or tie them to create either a functional closure or decorative-only
detail. If time is short, use these closure additions to revitalize an outdated ready-made favorite.

FIG. 6-10. Tabs, ties, and belts.

PATTERN AND DESIGN CONSIDERATIONS

Use the Designers' Template in the Appendix. Experiment by drawing tabs, ties, or belts in different arrangements, shapes, or sizes. For rhythmic repetition, duplicate the detail elsewhere on the garment or outfit, such as at the bottom of a pant leg or sleeve, over the top of a patch pocket, on the shoulder for a military-style epaulet, or across the back to draw in added fullness.

Experiment with proportion and determine the exact size, shape, and number of tabs, ties, or belts needed by cutting samples from paper and pinning them to a ready-made garment similar to the one you're constructing. When you've finalized the desired shape and size, add ¼" seam allowances to one of the paper samples to make a pattern.

CONSTRUCTION STEPS

The techniques to make tabs, ties, and belts are generally the same with a few minor differences. Ties are often more supple, made of lighter-weight fabric with no interfacing for easy tying capability. Belts and tabs are usually interfaced for added body.

General construction steps are described here, then special considerations specific to the detail follow (tabs, page 132; ties, page 134; belts, page 136). For variation, consider the double-tie construction option described on page 134, or make belts as a cut-on extension of the garment that is shaped into a belt (see Double-Front Extension, on page 136).

1. Cut two pieces for each tab or belt, using the newly created pattern. Because a tie closure includes two completed ties, cut four pieces for each tie closure.

2. When constructing tabs or belts, fuse mediumweight interfacing to the wrong side of one piece.

3. Stitch the pieces right sides together, leaving the end that will be stitched to the garment open for turning. If both ends are shaped or neither end will be sewn to the garment, leave 2" unstitched on a straight portion of the tab, tie, or belt. Take one stitch diagonally across corner points (Fig. 6-11).

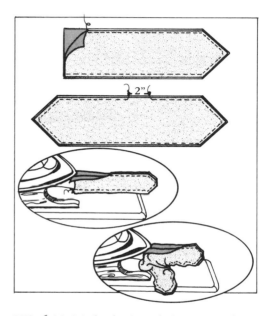

FIG. 6-11. Stitch tab, tie, or belt pieces right sides together, taking one stitch across corner points. Press seams flat, then press open.

4. Press the stitching flat on both sides. Then, for a crisp finish, press straight seams open over a point presser. Trim the seam allowances, clip the curves (if needed), and turn right side out through the opening. If the opening will be exposed, hand-blindstitch it closed.

5. If desired, topstitch each tab, tie, or belt ⅛" to ¼" from the edge. Refer to the following sections for various options on attaching the tabs, ties, or belts to the garment.

■ Tips on Tabs

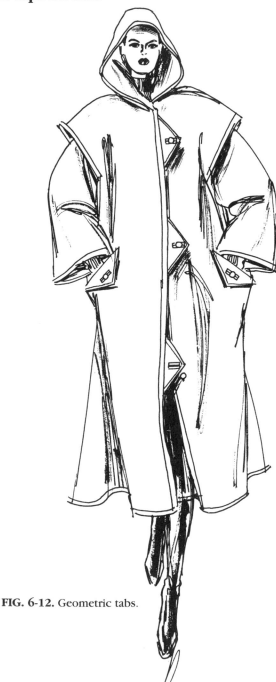

FIG. 6-12. Geometric tabs.

Design and construct the tabs following the instructions above. Geometric tabs with pocket flaps contoured to match are a favorite of ours (Fig. 6-12). Also consider duplicating tab shapes with pocket windows or pocket welts (Fig. 6-13). Consider the following options when attaching tabs to the garment.

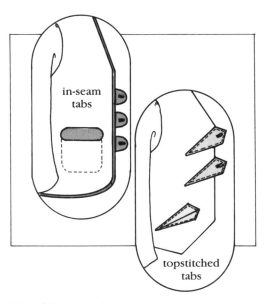

FIG. 6-13. Sew tabs into a seam or topstitch them to garment. Duplicate tab shapes for pocket windows or pocket welts.

■ Removable Tabs

Button or snap both ends for completely removable tabs (see Figure 6-10). Construct the garment following the pattern directions. Then try on the garment, position the tabs as desired, and mark the placement. Sew buttons and buttonholes or snaps to the garment and tabs as marked. Bound buttonholes are our favorite choice because they are easy to make and foolproof in such a small piece of fabric as a tab.

■ In-Seam Tabs

Attach one end of each tab to the garment by sewing it into a seam.

1. Construct the garment, leaving the seam unstitched where the tabs will be inserted. If desired, sew buttonholes in the tabs before attaching them to the garment.
2. Place the tabs to the garment, right sides together, with the unstitched end of the tab to the garment edge. Baste the unfinished edges together (Fig. 6-14).

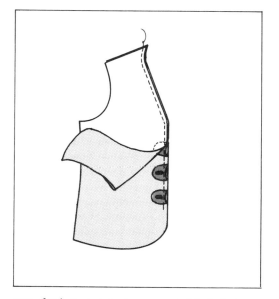

FIG. 6-14. Baste tabs to garment. Stitch facing to garment, sandwiching tabs between layers.

3. Position the other garment piece or facing to the original garment piece with right sides together, sandwiching the tabs between the layers. Sew the seam, stitching through both garment layers as well as the tabs.
4. Construct the rest of the garment. Try on the garment and mark the positioning of the tab closure. Sew buttons and buttonholes or snaps as marked.

■ Stitched-On Tabs

Attach one end of a tab by stitching it onto the garment. This option is the most versatile because the tab position is not limited to the loca-

tion of a seam. It can be attached anywhere on the garment, such as at the shoulder for an epaulet.

1. Construct the garment following the pattern guidesheet. Try on the garment and mark the desired position of the tab. If desired, sew buttonholes in the tabs before attaching them to the garment.
2. Zigzag or serge-finish the unfinished tab end.

✂ N O T E : If both ends of the tab are finished, consider topstitching the tab to the garment as shown in Figure 6-13.

3. Place the tab on the garment in the desired finished position as marked. Fold the tab back on the garment so right sides are together and the tab faces the opposite direction of the finished position (Fig. 6-15).

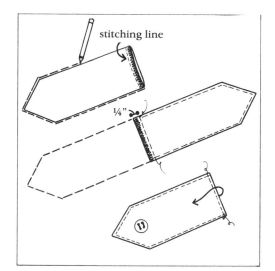

FIG. 6-15. Mark tab placement. Fold tab back and stitch open end to garment. Flip tab back and topstitch across end.

4. Attach the open end, stitching close to the finished edge. Flip the tab back to the finished position, and press. Topstitch across the end as shown in Figure 6-15.
5. Try on the garment and mark the positioning of the buttons and buttonholes or snaps. Sew the closure as marked.

■ Tips on Ties

FIG. 6-16. Tie closure variations: Grommets and ties, top-stitched double ties, banded-front with ties.

Design and construct the ties following the Construction Steps on page 131, or consider the Double-Tie Construction described below. In most cases, two ties are needed for each closure. One end of each tie is attached to the garment and the other is fastened to the other tie. The end attached to the garment can be stitched into a seam or onto the garment as for tabs in Figure 6-15. For a removable tie, work large grommets or buttonholes into the jacket front (Fig. 6-16).

The blouse with topstitched ties is ideal made with double ties. Make the ties extra long and stitch them across the blouse fronts before constructing the garment. The closure is secured with snaps; then the ties are knotted loosely over the opening. The banded-front blouse, also shown in Figure 6-16, has a center-front band with ties wrapped and stitched behind the band before the band is attached to the garment.

■ Double-Tie Construction

This novel tie option allows for two-toned construction. Two separate strips of fabric are seamed together then turned right side out to enclose the seam allowances. This technique is also ideal for fancy trim. If embellishing a curved edge, construct the trim using bias strips. Whether this technique is used to create trim or ties, it is an excellent method of combining two fabrics into one very interesting double tube.

1. Cut two strips for each tie. They may be different colors and different widths. For easy turning, choose silky or supple fabric.
2. Place the strips right sides together. If one strip is narrower, place it on top of the wider strip.
3. Fold the strips in half lengthwise, aligning the raw edges (Fig. 6-17). Seam the edges, being sure to catch all layers in the stitching.
4. Turn the strips right side out using your favorite method—a bodkin, bobby pin, needle and thread, Fasturn, or Loop Turner. *The turning device must be placed between the two thicknesses* so both layers are turned at the same time. Press the double tie flat. The two tubes are sewn together and the seam allowances are enclosed in one of the tubes.

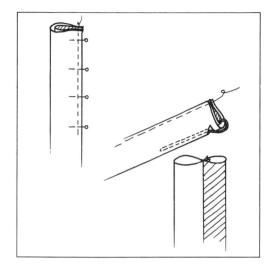

FIG. 6-17. Double-tie construction: Place strips right sides together and fold in half. Stitch, catching all layers. Turn by placing turning device between both thicknesses.

5. To attach the trim or ties to the garment, stitch in the ditch of the center seam. If the trim was made with wide tubes, you may need to stitch again on the outside edges to secure it to the garment.

■ Tips on Belts

FIG. 6-18. Belt closures: Cut-on belt and buckled tabs.

Here are two different options for constructing belt closures; choose your favorite or make up your own (Fig. 6-18). One is made with a tab-like extension sewn into the garment seam, and the other is made by reshaping the garment front and sewing it double layer to incorporate a belt extension.

■ Tab-Like Belts

For an easy-to-make belt closure, sew a tab-like extension to the garment. Design and construct the belt extensions following the Construction Steps on page 131. The end of the belt attached to the garment can be stitched into a seam or onto the garment as shown for tabs in Figure 6-15.

Overlap the garment fronts and wrap the belt toward the opposite side seam; then button or buckle it in place. For a buckle belt, you'll need to sew another tab-like extension into the side seam for attaching the other side of the buckle to the garment.

■ Double-Front Belt Extension

Double-front construction is ideal for this variation.

1. Trace the pattern to create separate right-front and left-front pattern pieces. Reshape the center-front edge of the right-front pattern piece to create the belt extension. Adjust the length of both front pattern pieces so the hem allowance is removed and just a seam allowance is extending past the hemline.
2. Cut two of each front pattern pieces (one for the inside layer and one for the outside layer). Sew the front pieces right sides together in sets of two, stitching at the center-front and lower edges and stopping ⅝″ from the ends (Fig. 6-19). Grade and clip the seam allowances, turn right side out, and press.

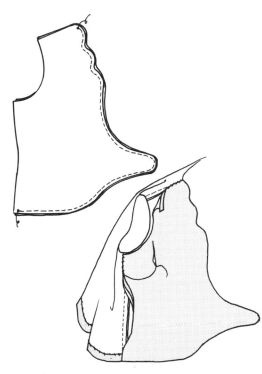

FIG. 6-19. Reshape center-front edge to create belt extension. Sew fronts right sides together. Turn right side out. Stitch shoulder and side seams, leaving inside layer unstitched. Hand tack inside layer.

3. Hem the lower edge of the garment back so the length of the side seam equals that of the front. Sew the front to the back, right sides together, at the shoulder and side seams, leaving the inside layer unstitched.

4. Press the shoulder and side seam allowances of the garment toward the front and press the shoulder and side seam allowances of the inside layer to the wrong side, as shown in Figure 6-19. Position the inside layer over the garment seam allowances and slipstitch.

■ BUTTONHOLE PATCHES

FIG. 6-20. Buttonhole patches.

A geometric dimension defines this closure with a splash of style (Fig. 6-20). Color-charged fabric patches lend a sporty spirit, while compatible colors in varying textures provide a more sophisticated statement.

■ PATTERN AND DESIGN CONSIDERATIONS

Choose any contrast-color or texture fabric for the patches. Leather, Ultraleather, and Ultrasuede are excellent choices: they have a unique texture and the ravel-free edges don't need turning. Use the patch fabric throughout the garment as a trim, pocket accent, or other detail.

To make the patch pattern, choose the button size for the garment. Draw a triangle, square, or circle at least ½″ larger than the button on all sides. Add a ¼″ seam allowance on all sides. If using leather or Ultrasuede, eliminate the seam allowance because the edges won't need turning under.

■ CONSTRUCTION STEPS

The patches under the buttonholes provide added stability that can replace buttonhole interfacing. In most cases, however, interfacing should still be used on the facing. To eliminate extra buttonhole bulk, use a medium to lightweight fabric.

1. Cut out the garment and patches. Press under ¼″ on all but one edge of each patch. If using another shape, press under all edges that will not be sewn into the garment seam.

✂ N O T E : To eliminate bulk, press-miter any corners where seam allowances intersect; then unfold the corner and trim away the excess seam allowance (Fig. 6-21).

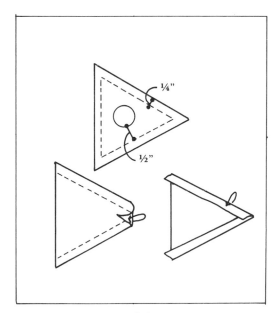

FIG. 6-21. Press under ¼″ seam allowances. Press-miter corner; then unfold and trim excess seam allowance to eliminate bulk.

2. Place the wrong side of the patches over the buttonhole placement marks on the right side of the garment's right front. Align the raw edge of the patch with the garment edge. Verify that the number of patches, size, and placement are pleasing for the garment. Then topstitch the patches in place.

3. Position and pin the facing and garment front right sides together, sandwiching the patches in between (Fig. 6-22). Sew the facing seam as pinned.

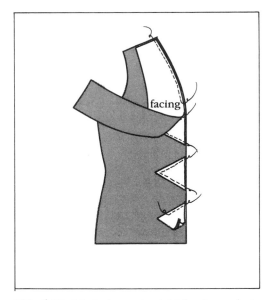

FIG. 6-22. Stitch shapes to right front over buttonhole placement marks; then stitch facing to garment front.

4. Complete the garment following the pattern guidesheet, using the modified front. Stitch the buttonhole through all layers including the patch.

■ DRAWSTRINGS

FIG. 6-23. Drawstring closures.

Decorative strands are pulled into a bow to create shirred folds of fabric (Fig. 6-23). Drawstrings are an ideal closure option which take you back in time for a romantic rendition while maintaining easy-fit construction.

■ DESIGN AND PATTERN CONSIDERATIONS

For a fuller, richer looking garment, choose a pattern that has added fullness, such as a bodice gathered into the shoulder or yoke seam or a skirt gathered at the waistline. If you have your heart set on a pattern that doesn't have enough fullness or if you want to add a drawstring to a part of the garment that is fitted, slash and spread the pattern to create your own fullness (Fig. 6-24).

Use the Designers' Template in the Appendix to experiment with drawstring closures in various arrangements. Duplicate drawstrings elsewhere on the garment to add additional closure

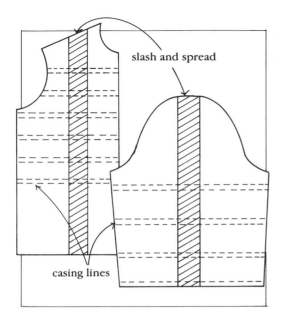

slash and spread

casing lines

FIG. 6-24. Slash and spread pattern to create added fullness; then mark casing placement lines.

or decorative-only details. A few options include the bottom of a pant leg, sleeve, or jacket, across the top of a patch pocket, around the neckline, along the shoulder seam, or up a skirt side seam for an asymmetrical hemline.

When designing your drawstring garment, decide whether you want the casings to be sewn to the inside or outside of the garment. If the casing will be stitched to the wrong side of the garment, you'll need buttonholes or grommets to allow the cord to tie on the right side.

Mark casing lines on the pattern to identify the location and finished width of the casing. The width of a casing may vary from ½″ to 2″ depending on the size of the cord, as well as the look you're trying to achieve. The casing ends will be approximately 1″ apart to allow room for the cords to tie. If the casing will be on the wrong side of the garment, mark grommet or buttonhole positioning.

>≈ N O T E : If the casing will be on the edge of the garment and made by folding the fabric edge (see Fig. 6-27), you must adjust the edge of the garment pattern to allow for the cut-on casing. Extend the pattern the exact width of the casing.

■ **CONSTRUCTION STEPS**

The two parts to a drawstring closure are the drawstring cord and the casing that the cord is drawn through. Each is constructed separately.

Cord Construction—The easiest option is to use a decorative cord purchased from your local fabric or craft store. Or you can make your own cording from a narrow fabric tube. To make the fabric tube, follow the instructions on page 45. Use straight-of-grain fabric strips for added stability. If using a Fasturn tube turner, consider making a corded tube (follow the manufacturer's instructions to do this).

Casing Construction—The technique used to construct the casing may depend on where the casing will be positioned on the garment. A topstitched casing can go anywhere on the garment, while an in-seam casing can only be positioned at a seam and a folded-edge casing can only be at the edge of a garment. For topstitched and in-seam casings, we recommend using the same fabric for the casings as used for the garment. If the fabric is too bulky, however, choose a lighter-weight compatible fabric for the casing.

TOP-STITCHED CASING (FIG. 6-25)

1. Measure the length of the casing lines on the pattern to calculate how much casing you need. Cut fabric strips the measured length plus ½″ by the finished casing width plus ½″. Press both long edges ¼″ to the wrong side.

2. Mark the casing lines on the garment; mark the side of the fabric where the casing will be stitched. If the casing is to run over garment seams, such as the bodice side seams, stitch those garment seams. Fuse the allowances down for easier threading of the drawstring cord.

3. Position and pin the wrong side of the casing to the garment. Turn the ends of the casing ¼″ to the wrong side and press. Sew the casing to the garment, topstitching along both long edges of the casing.

4. If the casing is sewn to the wrong side, insert grommets or stitch buttonholes where the cord will be brought to the right side as in Figure 6-25.

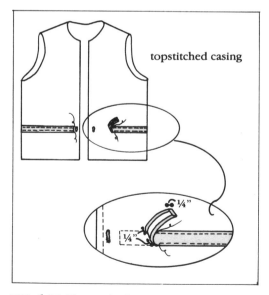

FIG. 6-25. Topstitched casing: Topstitch casing to garment. If casing is sewn to wrong side, sew buttonholes.

IN-SEAM CASING (FIG. 6-26)

1. Measure the length of the casing lines on the pattern to calculate how much casing you need. Cut fabric strips the finished casing width plus ¼″ and one seam allowance. For example, if you are making a 1″ casing and your pattern has ⅝″ seam allowances, you would cut the strips 1⅞″ wide (1″ + ¼″ + ⅝″). Press one long edge ¼″ to the wrong side.

2. If the casing is to run over garment seams, such as the side seams, stitch those garment seams before attaching the casing.

3. Position and pin the unfolded casing edge to the garment edge. For example, if the casing will be on the wrong side of the garment, position the wrong side of the casing to the wrong side of the garment.

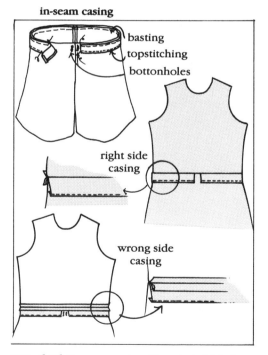

FIG. 6-26. In-seam casing: Topstitch folded edge of casing to garment. Stitch garment seam, catching casing in stitching.

4. Turn the short ends of the casing ¼″ to the wrong side and press. Baste the unfolded casing edge to the garment, stitching on the seamline. Topstitch the folded casing edge to the garment.
5. If the casing is sewn to the wrong side, insert grommets or stitch buttonholes where the cord will be brought to the right side.
6. Stitch the garment seam, catching the casing in the stitching.

FOLDED-EDGE CASING (FIGURE 6-27)

The folded-edge casing is usually stitched to the wrong side; otherwise the wrong side of the fabric will show on the right side of the garment.

1. Mark the casing fold lines on the garment. If the casing is to run over garment seams, such as the side seams, stitch those seams.

2. Fold the seam allowance to the wrong side and press. Fold the casing to the wrong side and press again.
3. Determine where the cord will be brought through to the right side of the garment and insert grommets or stitch buttonholes. Because the casing will be folded to the wrong side, the holes should go in the garment so the drawstrings can be drawn to the right side.
4. Pin the casing in place and topstitch the edge of the casing to the garment.

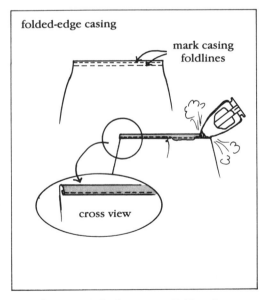

folded-edge casing

mark casing foldlines

cross view

FIG. 6-27. Folded-edge casing: Fold and press garment edge on seamline; then fold and press again on casing line. Topstitch casing to garment at folded edge.

■ Decorative-Only Drawstrings

FIG. 6-28. Decorative-only drawstrings.

This drawstring is not a closure, but a decorative option to correlate with a drawstring closure. It repeats the same shirring look as the drawstring above, but is constructed slightly differently, a novel accent to a shoulder seam or hemline (Fig. 6-28).

■ PATTERN AND DESIGN CONSIDERATIONS

1. Mark casing lines on the pattern to identify the location and finished width of the casing. The width of a casing may vary from 1″ to 2″ depending on the size of the cord, as well as

the look you're trying to achieve. The casing must be wide enough to accommodate two widths of cording (Fig. 6-29).

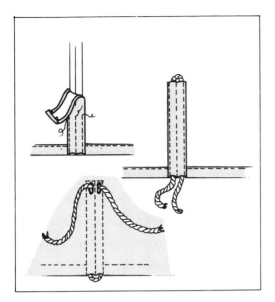

FIG. 6-29. Stitch casing to garment and draw cord through buttonholes, grommets, or open ends of casing.

2. If the casing will be stitched to the wrong side of the garment and the cords will be pulled to the right side, mark grommet or buttonhole positioning so the cord can be drawn to the right side. If the drawstring ties are at the hemline, as in the example illustrated in Figure 6-28, this step is not necessary.

■ **CONSTRUCTION STEPS**

1. Measure the casing lines on the pattern to calculate how much casing you need. Cut fabric strips the finished casing width plus ½". Press all four edges ¼" to the wrong side.

2. Mark the casing lines on the garment; mark the side of the fabric where the casing will be stitched. If the casing is to run over garment seams or hemline edges, stitch the seams and hem the edges before attaching the casing. If applicable, insert grommets or sew buttonholes as marked.

3. Position and pin the wrong side of the casing to the garment. Sew the casing to the garment, topstitching along each edge of the casing. Stitch again down the center of the casing.

■ Laced-Drawstring Variation

FIG. 6-30. Laced
drawstring variation.

Fashion flair defines this lace-up closure option,
an ideal variation for the front of a simple jewel
neckline or a low scoop back (Fig. 6-30). Also
use this technique to create a fancy skirt or pant
hemline, a stylish solution for too-tight pant
legs.

■ PATTERN AND DESIGN CONSIDERATIONS

1. Eliminate the seam where the lacing will be
added (if there is one) by marking the pattern piece so the seamline will be cut on the
fold. Mark the slit placement line at the foldline.

2. Make a facing pattern for the slit 2½″ wide
by the slit length plus 3″.

✄ N O T E : If you want to position the lacing on a seam,
such as at the bottom of a pant leg, extend the seam allowance 2″ at the slit and 3″ above the slit to create a
cut-on facing (Fig. 6-31).

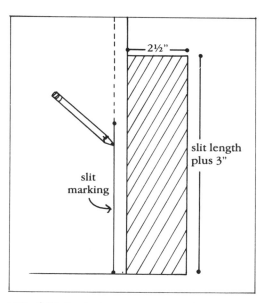

FIG. 6-31. For lacing on a seam, make a cut-on
facing by extending pattern 2½″ at slit.

3. If the lacing is at the neckline and your pattern has a neckline facing piece, combine the
neckline facing and the slit facing by overlapping the patterns and reshaping the outside
edge (Fig. 6-32). Mark the center edge of the
facing to be cut on the fold and transfer the
slit placement line from the garment pattern
to the facing pattern.

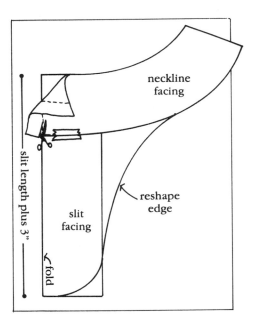

FIG. 6-32. For lacing at neckline, combine neckline facing and front-slit facing, overlapping patterns and reshaping outside edge.

■ CONSTRUCTION STEPS

1. Cut the garment out using the newly adjusted pattern pieces. Transfer the slit placement lines to the garment and facing. Fuse lightweight interfacing to the wrong side of the facing.

   If making the garment from knit fabric, fuse a 2"-wide strip of interfacing to the wrong side of the garment over the slit placement mark for added stability.

2. For neckline lacing, stitch the shoulder seams of the facing and garment. Finish the outside facing edge. Position the facing to the garment right sides together, matching the slit markings.

3. Staystitch around the slit marking, stitching through both layers and using a short stitch length (15 to 20 stitches per inch). Stitch the facing to the garment; then cut the slit, being careful not to cut through the stitching (Fig. 6-33). Turn the facing to the wrong side and

press. Edgestitch around the slit opening and neckline (if applicable).

4. If the slit is at a hemline, turn up and sew the hem. Trim the slit facing under the hem to reduce bulk. To eliminate bulk, consider facing the hem (combine the hem and slit facing as done for the neckline facing in Figure 6-32). Or consider binding the hem edge.

5. Mark the lacing holes on both sides of the slit approximately 1½" to 2" apart. Insert metal grommets or sew ⅜" buttonholes at the markings. (Be sure the grommets are large enough to support the drawstring).

6. Lace a long drawstring through the grommets or buttonholes. We used a 45" drawstring for an 8½" slit. Use a purchased cord or make your own drawstring by constructing a narrow fabric tube.

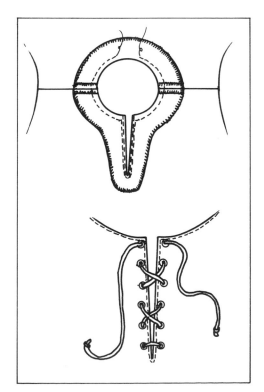

FIG. 6-33. Stitch facing to garment, turn to wrong side, then press and edgestitch. Insert grommets or sew buttonholes for lacing.

■ SHAPED EDGES

FIG. 6-34. Shaped closures.

Make wearable works of art by shaping the front button edges with curves and corners (Fig. 6-34). It's fun to change the shapes each time you sew the garment—make it up as you sew! For this improvising pattern work you can be dramatic, with exaggerated curves and corners, or subtle, with gradual lines to grace your particular figure.

■ PATTERN AND DESIGN CONSIDERATIONS

Shaped-edge closures are wonderful for all types of fabric and an assortment of garment styles. Consider drapery or upholstery fabrics for the more structured jackets or coat dresses.

Choose a simply shaped jacket, dress, or blouse pattern with a button-front closure. Consider the degree of wrap and how the extra fabric will look over your bustline. Use the Designers' Template in the Appendix to experiment, determining the shaped edges that please you most. This enjoyable exercise is valuable for creating lines that are pleasing to the figure; continually picture the body type of the one who will wear the garment.

To keep the original pattern intact, trace the bodice-front pattern; then work with the traced version. When you've decided on the finished look, reshape the front edge of the pattern using the template sketch as a guide. Relax while you shape the pattern, envisioning your sketches in full scale and adjusting for the ideal pattern shape.

■ CONSTRUCTION STEPS

Here are a few options for finishing shaped-edge closures:

Fitted Facings—Make fitted facings duplicating the front and hem edges of the bodice-front pattern pieces (Fig. 6-35). Remember to make

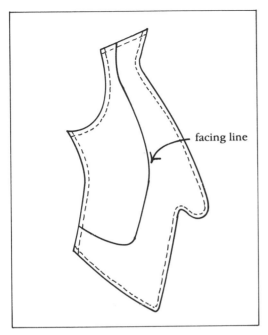

FIG. 6-35. Draw facing pattern to duplicate garment front and hem edges.

When stitching curves and corners, remember to shorten your stitch to strengthen the seam for trimming and clipping. Cut pie-shaped notches in the seam allowances of outside curves; cut clips in inside curves. (Use pinking shears for easy notches in outside curves.) Roll the seam to the underside and press carefully. For a crisp edge without an overpressed look, use a clapper in conjunction with steam pressing.

separate right and left facings for asymmetrical designs.

Double Front—A double front is often just as easy to make as a fitted facing. Follow the Construction Steps for the Cross-Front Closure on page 128, eliminating the steps for making the faced slits.

Bound Edges—Construct the garment single layer and bind the front, neckline, and hem edges. Use this option with a fabric that has enough body to support itself, or to create a soft, less constructed look. Button/buttonhole closures usually require the support of a facing and interfacing.

Double-front with Bound Edges—If you prefer the look of a bound edge, but need added body, try the double-front construction method except bind the front and hem edges instead of stitching them right sides together.

■ BUTTON-ON FASHION

FIG. 6-36. Button-on fashion.

Transform a long coat into a short one by buttoning off the lower section (Fig. 6-36). A row of decorative buttons remains to embellish the lower edge of a short coat. Garment parts that button on and off create dramatic style as well as functional versatility. Long full slacks can unbutton into cute cropped pants, while sleeve sections may button on or off at your whim. These "removable sections" can also be constructed so they don't actually come off, but are purely decorative.

■ Button-On Coat Bottom

A duster-style, loosely fitted coat pattern is perfect for the button-on variation shown in Figure 6-36.

1. Adjust the front and back pattern pieces by drawing a horizontal line (parallel to the hemline) above or below the fullest portion of the hip area (Fig. 6-37). This line must be

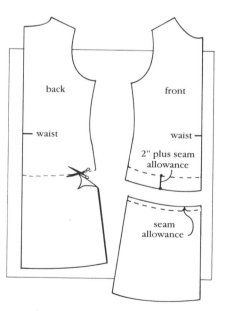

FIG. 6-37. Cut pattern apart above or below fullest hip area. Add seam allowances plus a 2″ underlap to newly cut edge of upper section. Add seam allowances to newly cut edge of lower section.

the same distance from the waistline on both the front and back pattern pieces.

2. Cut the patterns apart along the newly drawn cutting lines and add a seam allowance to the cut edge of the lower section. Add 2″ (for the button overlap/underlap) plus one seam allowance to the cut edge of the upper section.

3. Cut the coat from fashion fabric and lining fabric, using the adjusted pattern pieces. Construct the coat and lining separately, following the pattern guidesheet and leaving the hem unstitched. (Follow the construction steps for Button-Up Cuffs in the following procedure if you will be making cuffs.)

4. Place the coat and lining right sides together and stitch around the front and neckline edges. Stitch the hem edges together leaving a 6″ opening. Turn the coat right side out through the opening and press.

5. Hand stitch the hem opening closed and the lining to the coat at the sleeve hems. On the right side, sew buttons around the bottom edge of the upper coat.

6. Interface the upper edge of the lower coat to support the buttonhole area. Sew the coat bottom to the lining, right sides together, stitching all the way around the rectangle and leaving a 6″ opening. Turn right side out through the opening and press.

7. Sew buttonholes in the upper edge to line up with the buttons sewn to the upper coat.

■ Button-Up Cuffs

Oversized cuffs that button up are an ideal companion for the button-on bottom shown in Figure 6-36.

1. Use the coat sleeve pattern as a guide to draw a 10″ to 12″ cuff pattern (Fig. 6-38). Match the sleeve width at the base of the cuff, then flare the cuff 2″ to 3″ wider than the sleeve (1″ to 1½″ wider on each side).

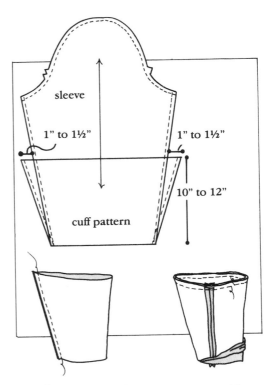

FIG. 6-38. Use coat sleeve pattern as a guide to draw cuff pattern. Flare cuff 2″ to 3″ wider than sleeve. Sew cuffs at upper edge; then turn right side out.

2. Cut four cuffs from fashion fabric. Seam each cuff into a circle. With right sides together sew two cuffs at the upper edge. Turn and press.

3. Place the right side of the doubled cuff to the wrong side of the coat sleeve, matching the raw edges of the sleeve with the raw edges of the cuff. Sew the layers together, stitching in a circle.

4. Sew one or more buttonholes into the top of the cuff and sew buttons onto the sleeve to correspond to the buttonholes. Or eliminate the buttonholes and sew the buttons to the cuff, stitching through to the sleeve. If desired, tack the cuffs at the underarm seam to hold them in place.

■ Button-On Bodice Front

FIG. 6-39. Button-on bodice front.

The lower portion of this blouse buttons to the upper yoke (Fig. 6-39). Choose a basic blouse pattern with set-in sleeves, preferably without princess seams or darts. The steps below use a button-front closure, but with a few modifications, you may use a blouse pattern with a back closure. For additional style, create a two-piece sleeve to correspond to the yoke line.

1. Cut the front pattern apart to create a yoke about 4″ to 6″ below the neckline (Fig. 6-40). Add a seam allowance to the cut edge of the lower section, and add 2″ (for the button

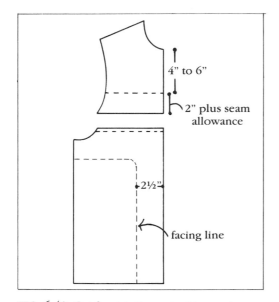

FIG. 6-40. Cut front pattern apart to create a yoke pattern. Add seam allowance plus 2″ underlap to yoke edge. Add seam allowance to upper edge of lower section. Draw fitted facing pattern for lower section.

overlap/underlap) plus a seam allowance to the lower edge of the yoke.

2. If desired, reshape the center-front yoke edge and the upper edge of the lower section into a scallop. Draw a 2½″-wide fitted facing for the lower section.
3. Cut four of the front yoke pattern. Sew one layer of the yoke to the back at the shoulders, right sides together. Sew the yoke lining to the back neckline facing at the shoulders, right sides together.
4. Place yoke and back piece to the lining and facing pieces, right sides together (Fig. 6-41). Stitch around the neckline, center-front, and lower yoke edges. Trim, clip, turn, and press. Topstitch if desired; then sew buttons at the lower-yoke edges.

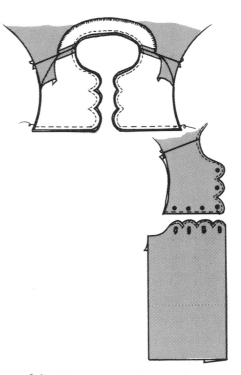

FIG. 6-41. Stitch yoke and back piece to lining and facing piece. Turn and topstitch. Sew buttonholes and buttons.

5. Cut two lower fronts and two fitted facings. Sew the facing to the bodice, right sides together, at the upper and center-front edges. Trim, clip, turn, and press. Topstitch if desired.
6. Sew buttonholes in the upper edge of the lower section; then button the lower front onto the yoke and construct the garment, treating the front as one. The armscye seam attaches the yoke to the lower portion so the lower half does not really button off completely.

■ DECORATIVE-ONLY CLOSURES

Overlapping button-seams or zipped closures can appear anywhere on the garment even when they won't be used for wearing purposes (Fig. 6-42). Non-closure options include pant legs, sleeves, skirt side seams, or princess seams—all surprising locations for unnecessary closures.

Button closures are easily created. On a straight seam, simply add 2½″ to both seam edges for a 2″ fold-back facing on each edge and an overlap/underlap. For shaped edges, add ½″ to each edge for the 1″ overlap, and cut a separate 2″-wide facing for each edge. No pattern changes are needed for zipped closures.

FIG. 6-42. Decorative-only button closure on pants.

■ **Tie-Back Opening**

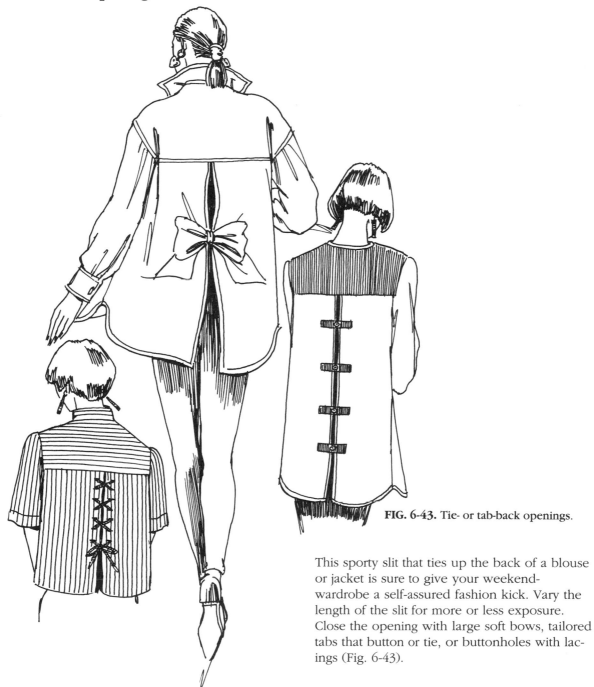

FIG. 6-43. Tie- or tab-back openings.

This sporty slit that ties up the back of a blouse or jacket is sure to give your weekend-wardrobe a self-assured fashion kick. Vary the length of the slit for more or less exposure. Close the opening with large soft bows, tailored tabs that button or tie, or buttonholes with lacings (Fig. 6-43).

■ **PATTERN AND DESIGN CONSIDERATIONS**

Begin with any free-hanging blouse or jacket pattern with a front closure. The traditional shirt-tail blouse is ideal for this styling.

1. Make a yoke seam by drawing a horizontal line (perpendicular to the grainline) 4″ to 8″ below the neckline at the center back (Fig. 6-44). For a longer slit, make the yoke closer to the neckline; for a shorter slit, make the yoke further from the neckline.

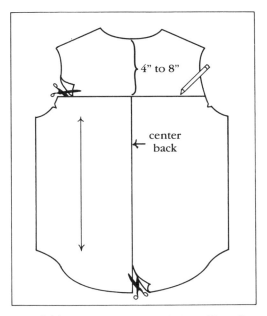

FIG. 6-44. Draw horizontal yoke line 4″ to 8″ below neckline. Draw center-back slit line parallel to grainline. Cut pattern apart.

2. Draw the center-back slit opening parallel to the grainline on the lower bodice piece.

3. Cut the pattern apart on the yoke and slit lines; then add seam allowances to the newly cut edges. Make a facing pattern 2½″ wide by the length of the slit opening (Fig. 6-45).

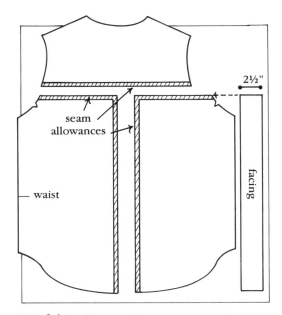

FIG. 6-45. Add seam allowances to newly cut edges. Make 2½″-wide facing same length as slit opening.

4. Determine the size and placement of the bows (or tabs). Ideal options include a single full bow positioned at the waistline, or three to four smaller bows (or tabs) evenly spaced down the slit. Draw the bow or tab pattern, using the guidelines shown in Figure 6-46; design your own.

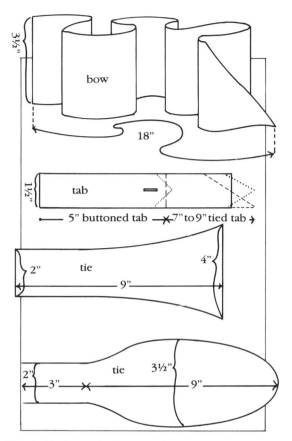

FIG. 6-46. Draw the bow or tab pattern as desired.

■ CONSTRUCTION STEPS

1. Cut one yoke, two lower backs, and two facing pieces from fashion fabric. Cut two facing pieces from interfacing.

2. Cut four tie or tab pieces for each closure (two ties are needed for each closure). For variety, use contrasting colored fabric for each closure to create an array of brights.

3. Stitch two tie pieces right sides together, leaving the end to be attached to the garment unstitched. Repeat for the remaining ties. Clip as needed; turn the ties right side out through the openings, and press.

4. Attach the interfacing to the back slit facings. Finish one long edge of each facing piece.

5. Pin the closures to the right side of the fabric at the slit edges, positioning them opposite each other on the left and right backs (Fig. 6-47). Align the raw edges and baste.

6. With right sides together, position the facings to the back bodice at the slit edges, sandwiching the ties between the facing and the bodice and aligning the unfinished edges. Stitch; then press the facing to the wrong side of the garment. Baste the facing in place at the hemline and upper edge.

7. Position the lower bodice pieces to the yoke, right sides together, matching the top of the slit with the center back of the yoke, as shown in Figure 6-47. Stitch, then press the allowances toward the yoke.

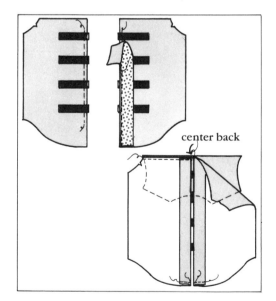

FIG. 6-47. Position facings to back bodice, sandwiching ties or tabs between facing and bodice. Stitch; then sew lower bodice pieces to yoke.

8. Complete the garment following the pattern guidesheet, using the completed tie-back bodice. If making tabs that will button closed, refer to the Design and Sew Tip on page 49, for Nearly Perfect Buttonholes.

■ Lacing Option

For the lacing option, follow the previous construction tips through Step 6, eliminating the bow or tab closures. Before sewing the lower bodice to the yoke, sew buttonholes or insert grommets through the garment and facing layers. Space them 1½" to 2" apart from the top of the slit to the waistline, positioning them ½" from the edge on both sides of the slit. Finish Steps 7 and 8 of the above procedure; then lace a long fancy cord from top to bottom through the buttonholes or grommets.

■ **Keyhole Variation** (Figure 6-48)

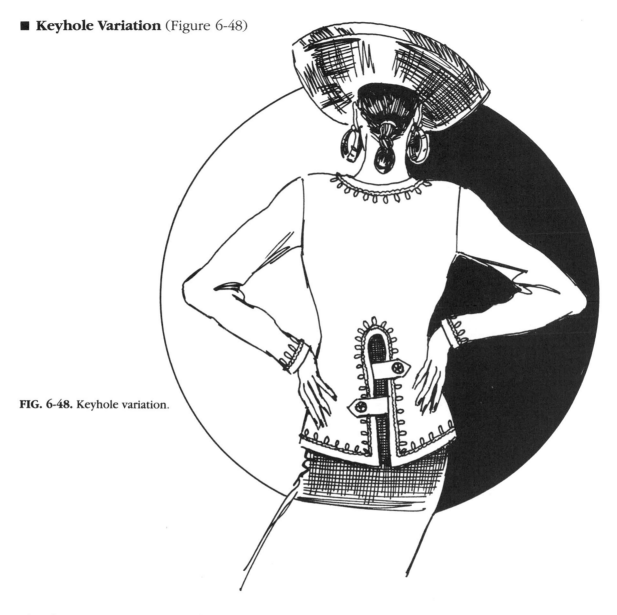

FIG. 6-48. Keyhole variation.

This dramatic variation adds a flirty touch to blouses, vests, or jackets. This time the slit rounds at the top and drops to the hemline; a shaped hemline looks stunning with this variation.

1. Draw the keyhole at the center back, beginning at the lower edge of the back bodice pattern. It should be approximately 11″ long, depending on the length of your garment. The broadest portion of the keyhole is 1½″

to 2″ wide. Draw a ½″ seam allowance; then cut the keyhole opening in the pattern.

2. Cut four tab pieces 2½″ wide by 4½″ long with a point at one end. Stitch two pieces right sides together, leaving the squared end unstitched. Clip the corners, turn right side out, and press. Repeat for the other two tab pieces.

3. Position the tabs to the right side of the fabric at the keyhole, so when they are opened out, they will wrap across the finished slit in different directions (Fig. 6-49). Align the raw edges and baste the tabs in position.

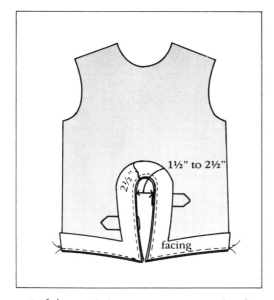

1½" to 2½"

2½"

facing

FIG. 6-49. Stitch facing to garment, sandwiching tabs between.

4. Use the adjusted back bodice pattern as a guide to make a 2½″-wide shaped facing for the keyhole and hemline edges. Cut one facing, interface the keyhole portion of the facing, and finish the outside facing edge.

5. Position and stitch the facing to the garment, right sides together, sandwiching the tabs between. (See Figure 6-49.) Trim the corners

and clip inside the keyhole curve. Press the facing to the wrong side.

ENDLESS OPTIONS
Enclose piping in the center-back opening seam. Decorative topstitching along the hem and around the opening holds the facing in place; our favorite is done with a heavier-weight decorative thread in the bobbin and stitched wrong side up. Bind the outside edges with contrast bias binding or accentuate the detail with trims or braids. If a straight-slit opening or keyhole shape is too plain for you, try a more dramatic shape at the top of the opening such as a heart or clover.

Thank you for sharing with us our passion for designing and sewing clothes. For most of our lives, we have been captivated with designing and sewing our own wardrobes as well as teaching and writing about sewing. It has been our great pleasure to share this love with you. We hope we have stimulated creative fashion ideas within you so the garments you design have a fresh innovative look. We're confident that the wonderful details you add to each design will prompt multiple compliments and make your one-of-a-kind garments better than ready-to-wear at any price point.

Consider your lifestyle, wardrobe needs, and available time as you choose garment styles and details you want to design and sew. Each idea in this book is easily manageable with a relatively small amount of pattern work and sewing time. If you're unsure about a style, test it out in inexpensive fabric or muslin before incorporating it into a garment.

We feel very fortunate to be surrounded by many wonderful sewing friends, a network of people with whom we enjoy consulting and sharing ideas. Perhaps you do not have such a design and sewing group of friends available to you, and if not, consider us those friends. Please send us a note to let us know about your latest projects or any comments you may have about this book.

Living in the San Francisco Bay Area, we are exposed to and feel free to experiment with many varied styles and trends. We encourage you to design and sew at least one new look each season. Be bold about trying new styles, creating works of art on the fashion forefront. Friends will look to you for a refreshing fashion story. While we are not slaves to fashion trends, it is fun to change the way we dress, adapting a new style to a wearable look that fits our unique lifestyles.

Our last and most important request is that you enjoy experimenting with the ideas in this book. Do "Make It Your Own!"

■ DESIGNERS' TEMPLATES

These blank figure drawings allow you to practice sketching garment designs while keeping proportions accurate. Designing with a pencil before carrying it to fabric is invaluable. By sketching your ideas, you can create as daring or outrageous designs as you like without taking the risk or incurring the costs of making a design that doesn't suit you or your fabric. Here are some ideas on using the templates:

■ Photocopy the templates as many times as you like. Leave the templates in the book unmarked so you'll always have a fresh template to copy.

■ Draw the basic garment without sketching design details; then make a number of copies of the garment sketch. Now you can practice drawing many variations of the design detail on the garment without having to redraw the garment each time.

■ Keep a few blank copies on hand when you go shopping. If you see a design you want to remember, you can quickly jot it down onto the template without having to worry about your figure-drawing skills.

■ Keep a notebook of your template sketches. Flip through the notebook periodically; you'll be pleasantly surprised at how one idea can inspire many others.

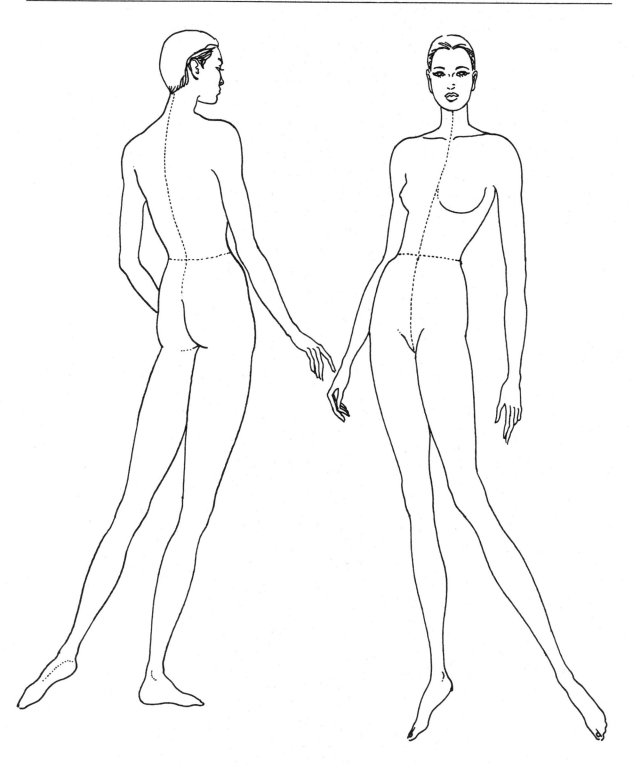

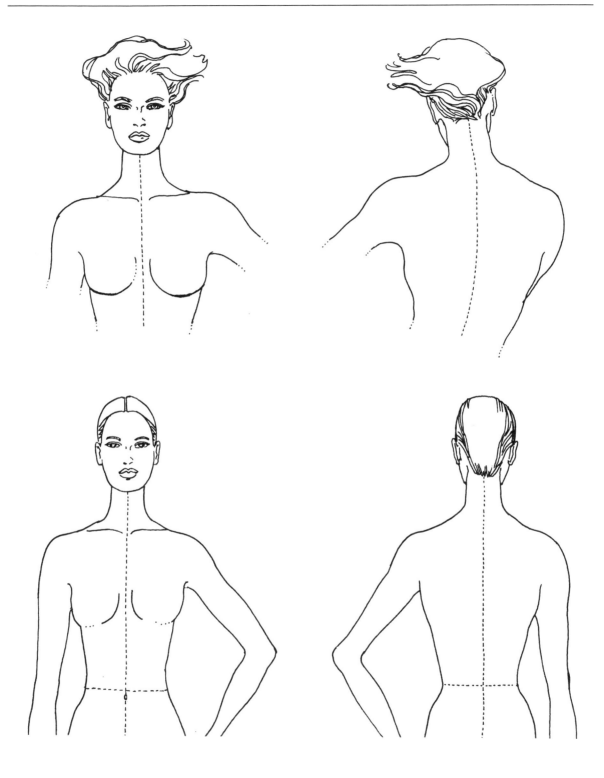

Ronda Chaney is the chairperson and a professor for the Fashion Design and Textiles Department at Cañada College in Redwood City, CA. Her creativity and sense of design combined with her enthusiasm for sewing have inspired many students to uniquely express their own creativity through fabric and fashion.

In addition to her work at Cañada, she instructs at a number of sewing schools, lectures at various sewing events, is a freelance writer, and consults for community fashion programs and private clothing businesses. Ronda studied textiles and clothing at San Francisco State University, where she received a Masters of Science Degree in home economics. Before that, she studied at the University of Missouri, where she graduated with a Bachelor of Science Degree also in home economics.

Amidst her busy schedule, Ronda still manages to escape to her sewing room and create wonderful additions to her wardrobe of unique designs. She lives in Redwood City, CA, with her husband, Lon, and the two of them enjoy excursions to the mountains for backpacking getaways.

Lori Bottom is a writer for national sewing publications, and is the author of *Taming Your First Serger* and co-author of *ABCs of Serging*. She studied fashion design and textile science at California Polytechnic State University (San Luis Obispo), where she graduated with a Bachelor of Science Degree in home economics. Lori's passion for sewing combined with her attention to detail are an ideal combination for her writing career.

Previously, Lori was an editor on the *Update Newsletters* staff. Currently, in addition to her freelance writing, she works for Nestlé Beverage Company, coordinating the support and documentation of business computer systems.

As a lifelong sewing enthusiast, Lori cherishes her creative time, sewing for herself, her home, and others. She lives in San Anselmo, CA, with her husband, David Tanzer, and a menagerie of animals. Together, she and her husband enjoy traveling around the country in their small airplane.